great spaces
SMALL HOUSES

great spaces
SMALL HOUSES

great spaces SMALL HOUSES

Author: Daniel González

Publishers: Carles Broto

Graphic Design: Albert Valero

Production: Jorge Carmona

Editorial Coordinator: Jacobo Krauel

Architectural Adviser: Pilar Chueca

Text: Contributed by the architects, edited by Jacobo Krauel and Amber Ockrassa

Photo cover: © H. Abadie

© Carles Broto i Comerma
Jonqueres, 10, 1-5
08003 Barcelona, Spain
Tel.: +34 93 301 21 99 Fax: +34-93-301 00 21
E-mail: info@linksbooks.net

Printed in Barcelona, Spain

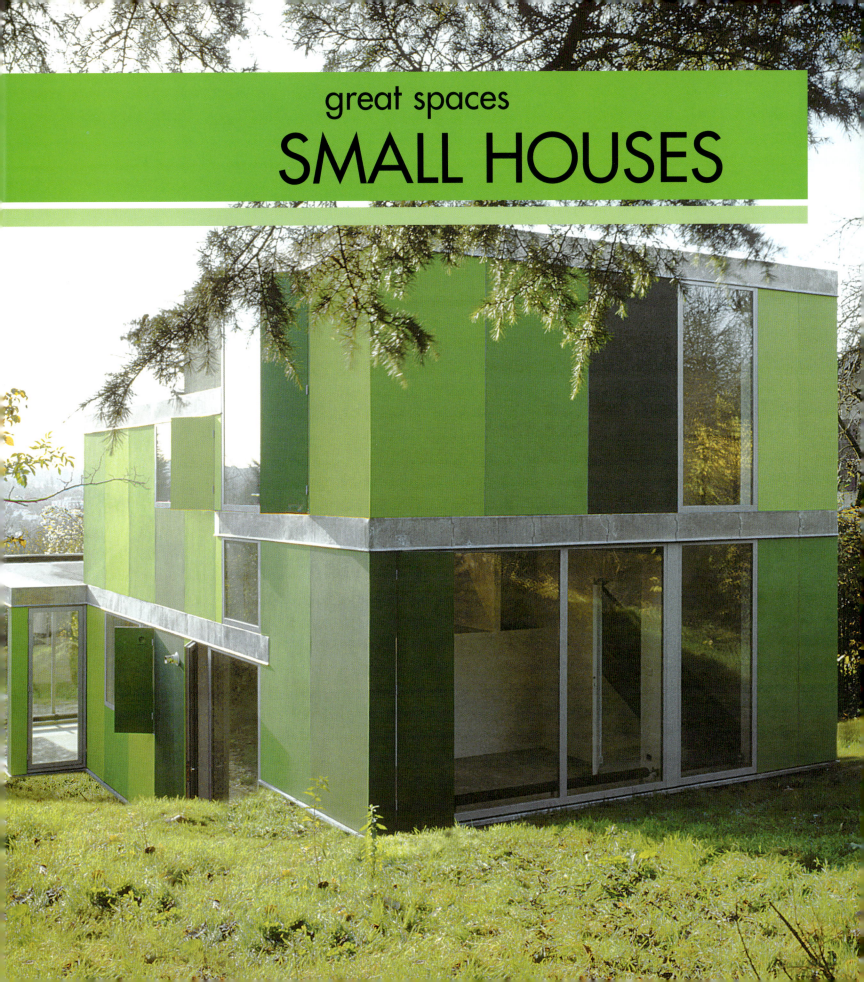

great spaces
SMALL HOUSES

INDEX

10 MVRDV
Borneo House

22 Mutsue Hayakusa
(Cell Space Architects)
House in Motoazabu

32 Robert Oshatz
Gibson Boathouse/Studio

42 Markus Wespi
& Jérôme de Meuron
House in Flawil

50 Jo Crepain Architect NV
Water-tower

60 Eduardo Souto de Moura
Casa Baiâo

66 Niall McLaughlin
Northamptonshire Shack

76 Arnaud Goujon Architecte DPLG
Transformed penthouse

86 Gray Organschi
Tennis House

96 de Architectengroep
(Dick van Gameren & Bjarne Mastenbroek)
Apartments in a sewage plant

104 Sean Godsell
Carter / Tucker House

114 Satoshi Okada Architects
Villa Man-Bow

124 José Gigante
Wind Mill Conversion

132 Marin-Trottin
Péripheriqués Architectes
MR House

144 Philip Gumuchdjian
D.P. Think Tank / Boathouse

152 Takao Shiotsuka
Shigemi House

162 Daniele Marques & Bruno Zurkirchen
Haus Kraan Lang

172 Shigeru Ban
Paper House

178 Flemming Skude
Con Cave

186 Francesco Venezia
House in Posillipo

192 Shin Takamatsu & Associates
Iwai House

202 Alvaro Siza
Figueiredo House

210 Mauro Galantino & Federico Poli (Studio3)
Casa sul lago d'Orta

222 Mutsue Hayakusa (Cell Space Architects)
Fold House

234 Silvia Gmür & Livio Vacchini
3 Single-Family Houses

246 Takao Shiotsuka
N Guest House

INTRODUCTION

Great architectural works are not necessarily those that are measured by the number of square meters. Creation depends on the space and the possibilities that it affords. Therefore, architectural work in small spaces is often a challenge in which one must achieve the seemingly impossible: to turn a small space into a comfortable dwelling in which the lack of living space is not perceived.

The aim of this book is to show those designs that stand out for their skill in creating stimulating environments in small spaces. This is a complicated task that is not limited to removing partitions, building mezzanines and incorporating specific furniture for the needs of the space. A skillful use of a small space requires far more: one must also think of the requirements and the comfort of the clients, and devise an aesthetic design in which the architecture can adapt to the restrictions of a limited floor area. A total of 26 works show the imaginative force of the designs in which small premises can be transformed into comfortable dwellings, regardless of their original use or location.

The designs include apartments created after the division of a large flat, small single-family dwellings in the country and terraced fantasy dwellings. They are complemented by plans and explanations of the architectural work carried out in each scheme, all of which is proof positive that creative design does not depend on the available floor space.

MVRDV
Borneo House

Amsterdam, The Netherlands

In Borneo (Sporenburg) one dwelling stands out because of its resolution and the great spatial possibilities applied within the constraints of its limited size. Located on plot 18, the home is 4.2 meters wide and 16 meters high and has a spacious double-height terrace on the facade facing the water. Initially the regulations only allowed the construction of three floors: a high floor at street level and two more above it. Despite this, the architects were able to build four floors by building in blocks and setting one of the four levels at the rear. A long traverse section was also designed with two "closed" elements: a space with direct access to the street that serves as a garage, and another block suspended over the terrace and the water on the second level that stands out from the rest of the building and houses the bedroom and a bathroom.

The remaining irregular space of the house —the kitchen-dining room, the living room and the study— are communicated so as to provide a fluid and simple transition from one room to the next. The rooms were designed with different heights and degrees of privacy. Each one is directly connected to the exterior through an exclusive access, with the double height terrace, an overhanging window and a roof garden aligned in the rear facade.

Photographs: Nicholas Kane

Perspective

The use of displaced volumes gives this dwelling a large, double-height space, half of which is a covered terrace looking onto the canal.

Elevation streetside

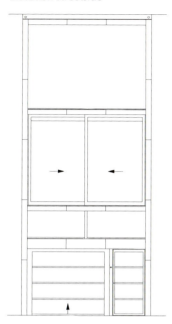

Elevation waterside

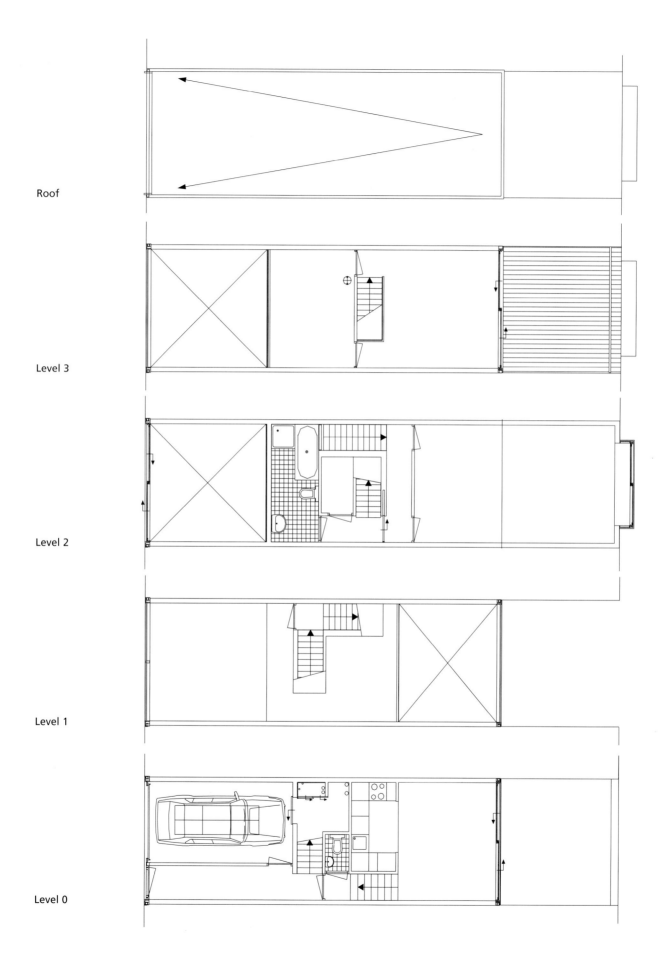

Roof

Level 3

Level 2

Level 1

Level 0

17

Sections

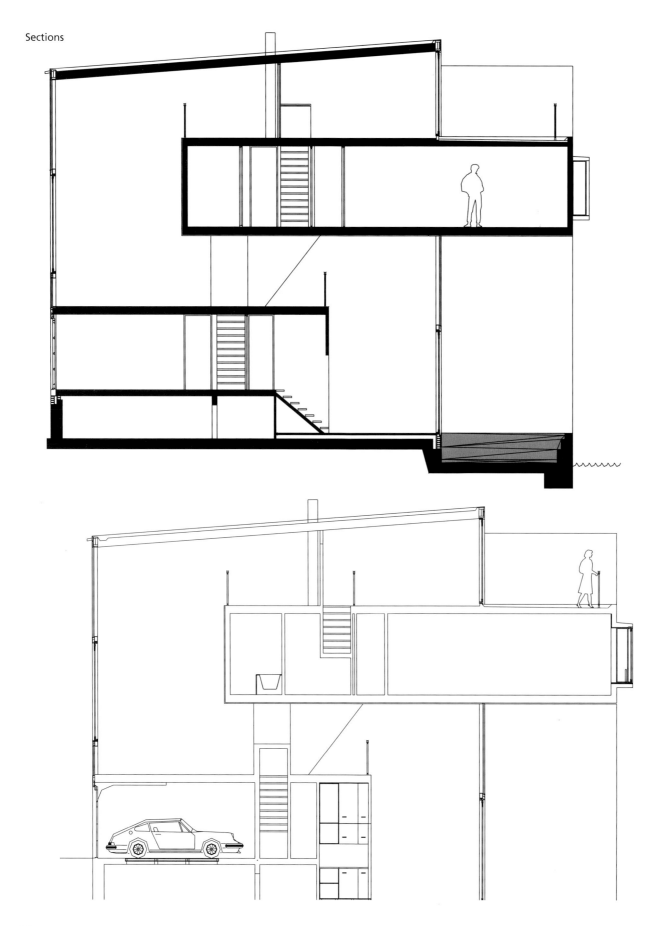

The typology of the spaces is determined by the interplay between the vertical nature of the building and the horizontal elements in its interior, and by the natural lighting.

Mutsue Hayakusa (Cell Space Architects)
House in Motoazabu

Tokyo, Japan

Designed for a couple in their fifties, this small residence consists of three floors joined by a spiral staircase. Because the site is small with an unusual shape, the design team has explored new options by using alternate angles and contrast.

The garage and the entrance are divided by curved glass, which gives an expanded reflection and creates the illusion of space so necessary on this restricted site. The white floor of the garage is used to reflect natural light into the home. The client's car in the garage is reflected by the mirror onto the entrance ceiling, thereby enhancing the feeling of spaciousness.

As the home has been designed for an elderly couple one of the important considerations was that it should allow for easy wheelchair access.

The home has an elevator located near the entrance.

In the bedroom, soft natural light from the balcony is filtered through louvers. The space is flexible and can be adjusted to suit varying needs and preferences.

Carved movable partitions clad in silver Japanese paper can be moved to divide the room. A closet mirror visually broadens the space. The entire living space is ensconced in softly pleated wooden walls and ceilings.

The hard image of the exterior view is broken on the third floor by willow louvers. The window reflects the pleated wooden wall at night and visually extends the space.

The kitchen and dining room comprise a single, brightly-lit space.

Photographs: Satoshi Asakawa / Katsuhisa Kida

Site plan

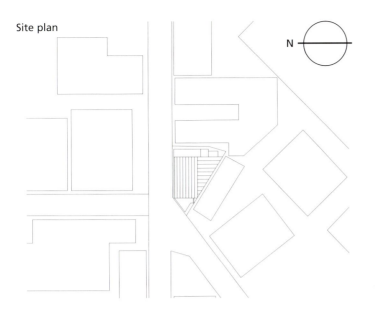

The curved glass separating the garage from the entrance gives an expanded reflection and creates an illusion of increased space. The white floor of the garage is used to reflect natural light into the home. The car in the garage is also reflected in the mirror on the entrance ceiling, further enhancing the feeling of spaciousness.

First floor plan

1 Entrance
2 Garage
3 Elevator

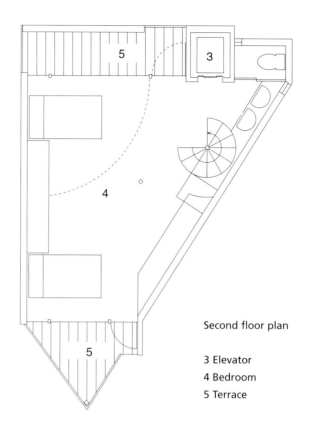

Second floor plan

3 Elevator
4 Bedroom
5 Terrace

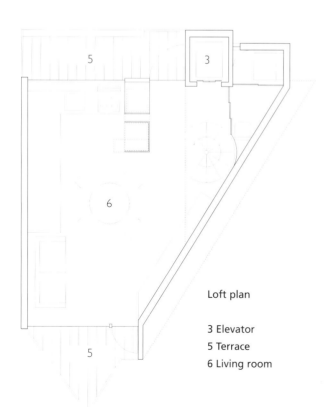

Loft plan

3 Elevator
5 Terrace
6 Living room

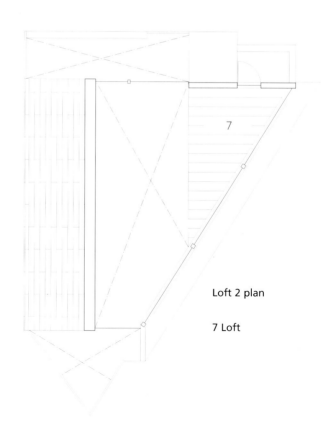

Loft 2 plan

7 Loft

Section 1   1 Living room
2 Bedroom
3 Garage

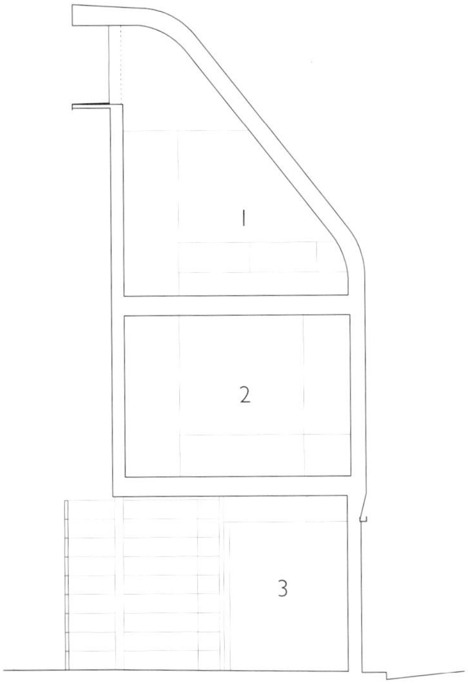

North elevation

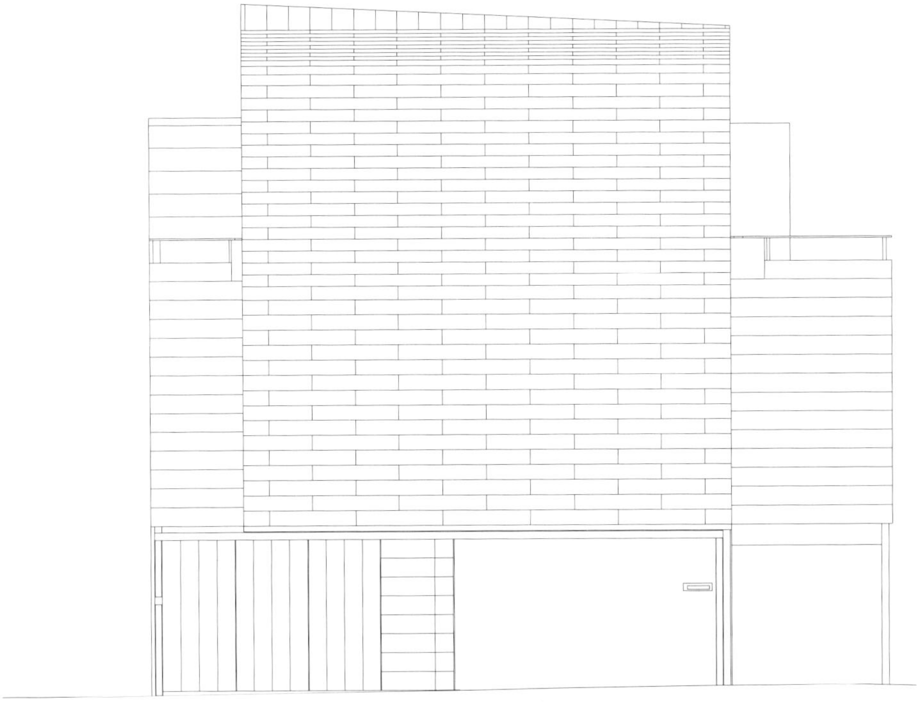

Carved movable partitions clad in silver Japanese paper can be moved to divide the bedroom. A closet mirror visually broadens the space. The entire living space is ensconced in softly pleated wooden walls and ceilings.

Section 2   1 Living room
2 Loft
3 Bedroom
4 Entrance
5 Garage

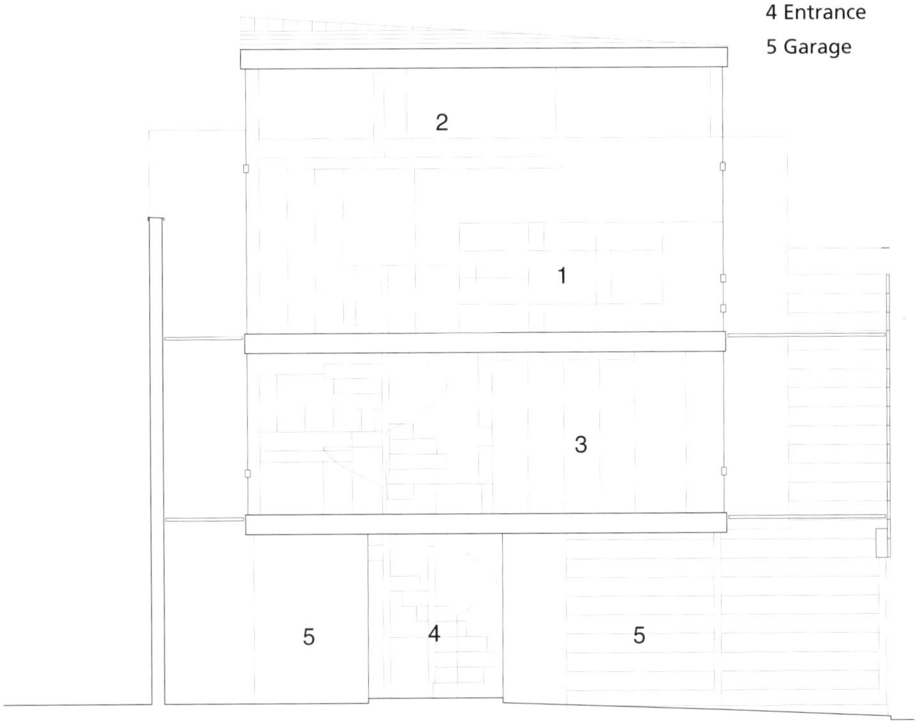

Robert Oshatz
Gibson Boathouse/Studio

Lake Oswego, Oregon, USA

The Gibson's had an existing boathouse but felt it was a blemish on their property. They wanted to reuse the existing boat stall but build a new boathouse while adding a new studio and study. The site went from the lake up the hillside to the driveway above. Since the driveway to their property is shared with neighbours, it was decided to build the studio into the hillside and have a sod roof so the structure would not be noticed as the neighbor drove down the driveway. Mrs. Gibson, an artist, wanted her studio space to have high ceilings and ample natural light. Mr. Gibson, an entrepreneur, wanted a more intimate space to keep track of his business activities. The structure grows out of stonewalls that are shaded by an arching sod roof. The roof is constructed with straight Douglas fir glue-laminated beams and fir decking.

Photographs: Robert Oshatz

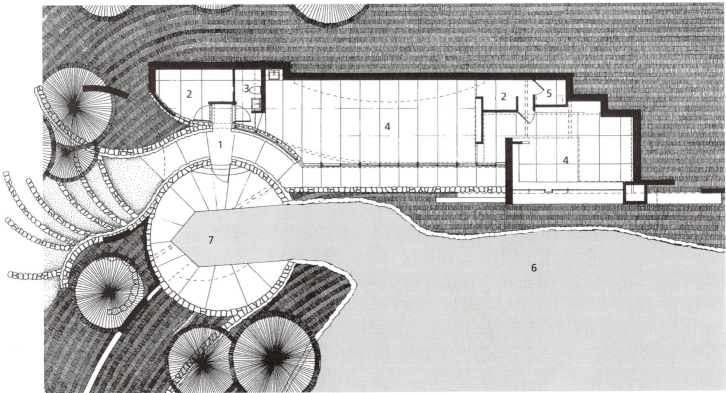

Floor plan
1. Entry walk 2. Storage 3. Toilet 4. Study 5. Vault 6. Lake Oswego 7. Boathouse

South-west elevation

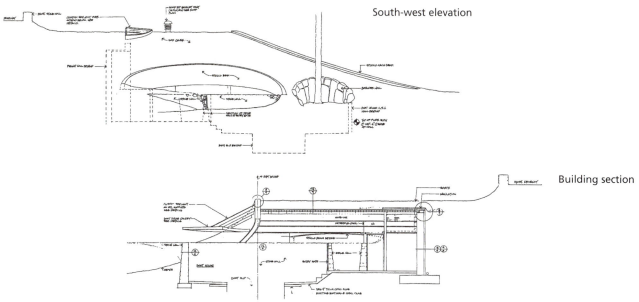

Building section

The idea of building a studio in the jetty area added a privileged space to the dwelling. It is camouflaged by the vegetation-covered roof, which hides it from the passers-by who use the path leading to the other houses.

Sections

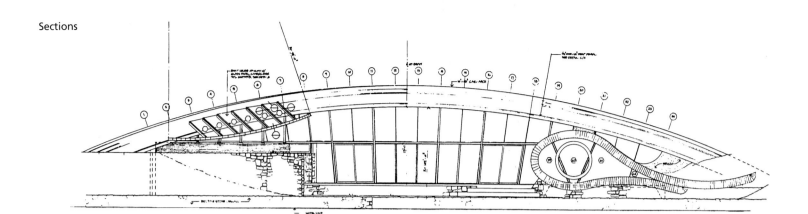
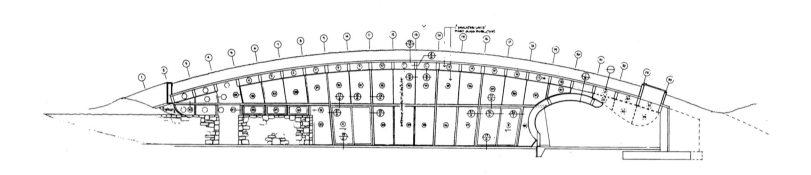
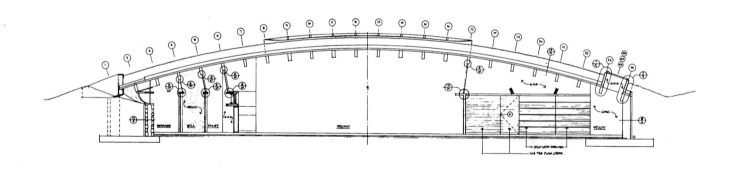
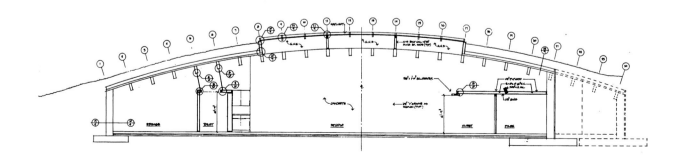

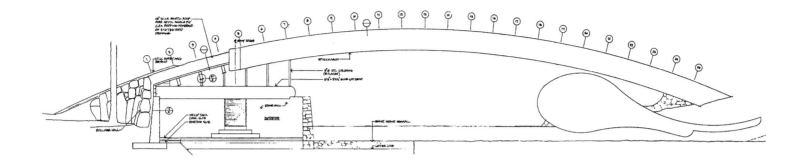

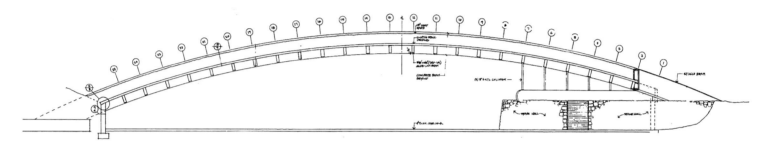

Sections

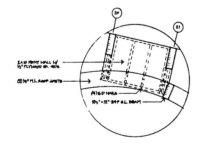

Pony wall from arch to roof

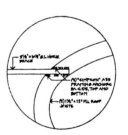

Transom to arch detail

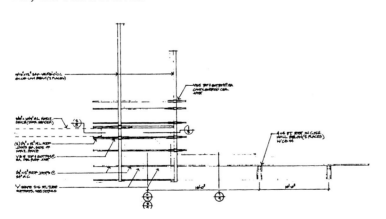

Study roof frame plan

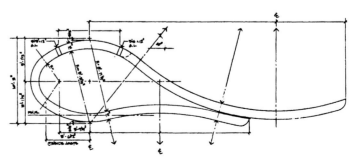

Study arch frame detail

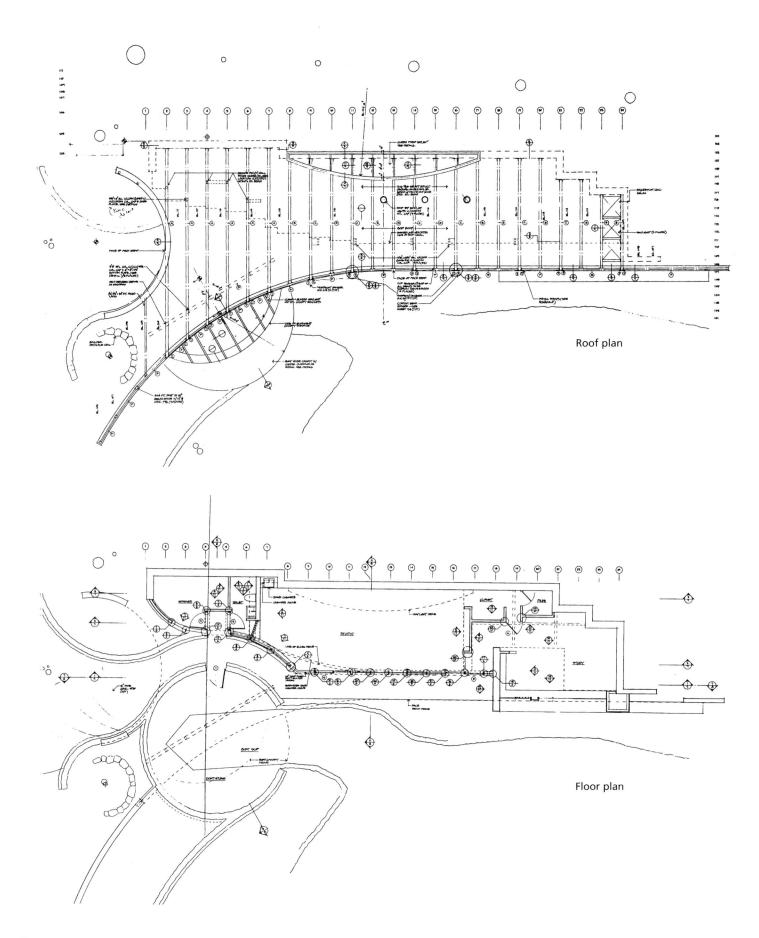

Roof plan

Floor plan

The main elements used in this scheme (stone, wood and glass) are completely ecological and maintain a pleasant relationship with the surroundings of the studio-jetty. A skylight in the vegetation-covered roof provides toplighting for the interior of the studio.

Markus Wespi & Jérôme de Meuron
House in Flawil

Flawil, Switzerland

Although not immediately visible from the exterior, a closer inspection of this house revealed that it was one of the first prefabricated timber constructions in Switzerland. It is located in an agricultural area where wood has been used extensively in building construction.

The original outer rendering was entirely removed, to be replaced with slats of Douglas fir wood as exterior cladding and insulation all around the house. On the windowless facades, the slats have been placed closely together, while only every third slat was included on the south facade in order to let in views and light. Wood was also used extensively in the interior in order to create a sense of unity, while the roof was replaced with titanium-zinc sheeting.

Although the existing house was very small, the conversion extended it by only 1.5 meters to the south. In the process, the entire south facade was removed and replaced with large windows. Since the other three facades remained closed, the decision was made to harness some of the passive solar energy along the south facade.

A secondary road passes directly in front of the house, so the wooden slats provide a screen for preserving privacy, while also serving as solar protection in the summertime.

From a distance, the house seems to be a completely hermetic structure. In its simplicity, it is reminiscent of the traditional barns so common in this canton.

New insulation, central gas heating and a warm-air stack were installed. The original timber stud walls and concrete plinth were retained. The existing fir flooring on the upper floor was also retained, while parquet was added on the ground floor.

A covered bicycle stand and wood shelter are new additions in the garden.

Photographs: Hannes Henz

Section AA Section BB

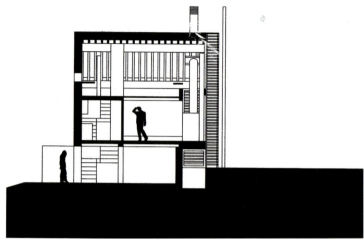

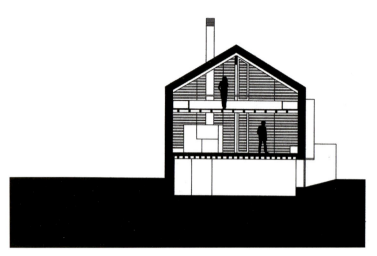

1. Covered bicycle stand
2. Garden
3. Entrance
4. Bath-toilet
5. Guestroom
6. Storage
7. Heating-washroom
8. Kitchen/dining room
9. Living room
10. Chimney
11. Study
12. Bedroom
13. Void

Although the end result of the renovation has the look of an almost entirely new construction, certain elements of the existing structure were retained: the original timber stud walls, concrete plinth and timber flooring, for example. Pictured here, the house in its original state.

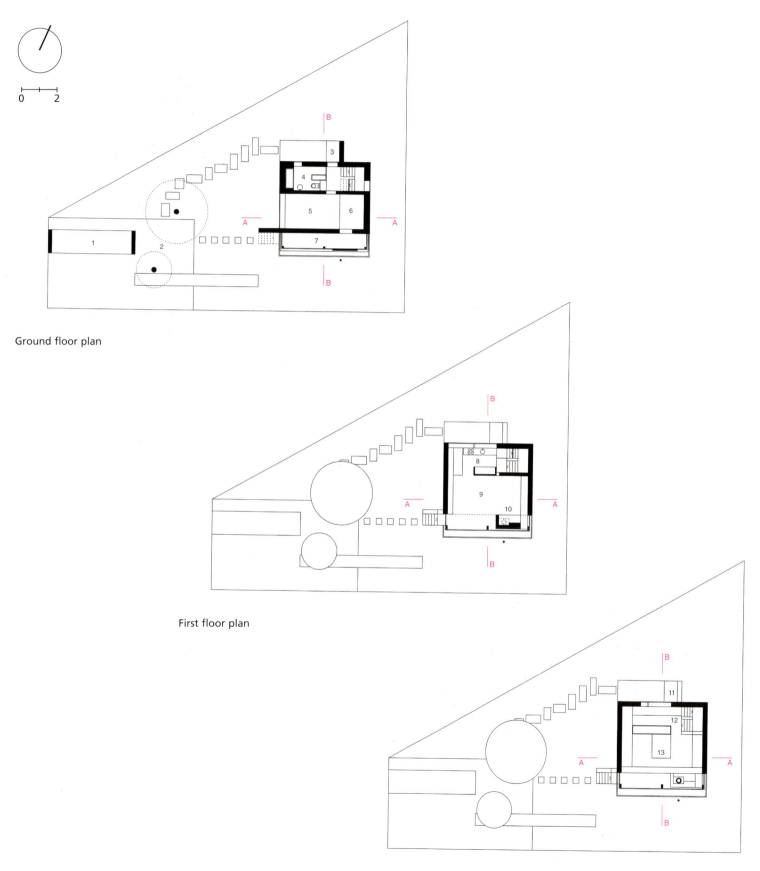

Ground floor plan

First floor plan

Second floor plan

The renovation involved creating a new front entrance, eliminating some of the windows and stripping the original structure's exterior rendering. The roof was replaced by titanium-zinc sheeting, while all exterior walls are clad in Douglas fir slats. The spacing of the slats on the south facade creates a sun shade and a screen for privacy within the home.

Jo Crepain Architect NV
Water-tower

Brasschaat, Belgium

Until 1937, this water tower with a height of over 23 meters was used to provide water to the castle and other buildings of the county of Brasschat, near the city of Antwerp. After being in disuse for decades due to the construction of four new water tanks and the planning of a modern water supply system, it survived a planned demolition. The conservation of this peculiar cylindrical tower crowned by a large, four-meter-high cistern allowed it to be converted into an unusual single-family dwelling. The architect respected the original industrial typology, leaving the four large pillars that sustain the structure exposed, and also maintained the compositional structure and the essential functionality of the original design. This was achieved by minimizing the presence of decorative objects and by limiting the elements and materials to reinforced concrete, structural glass and galvanized metal. Around the original structure, a parallelepiped, double-height volume with a mezzanine surrounds the tower at ground level. This new construction houses the services and a living room that is totally open and transparent to the exterior. This breaks the verticality of the scheme and gains space, and its roof acts as a terrace for the first floor, which houses the main bedroom.

The new tower achieves its maximum expressiveness when it is illuminated at night. The transparency of the glass structure that wraps the building allows the occupants to enjoy the wooded landscape with a small winding creek and reveals the three floors of 4x4 m, each with a small balcony. These floors house, from bottom to top, the study, the guest bedroom and a small winter garden. At the top of the tower the water cistern is conserved, now transformed into a curious space without windows that is intended for private receptions.

Photographs: Sven Everaert/Ludo Noël

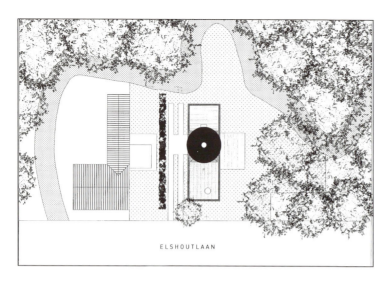

Site plan

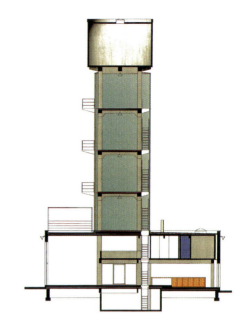

Section

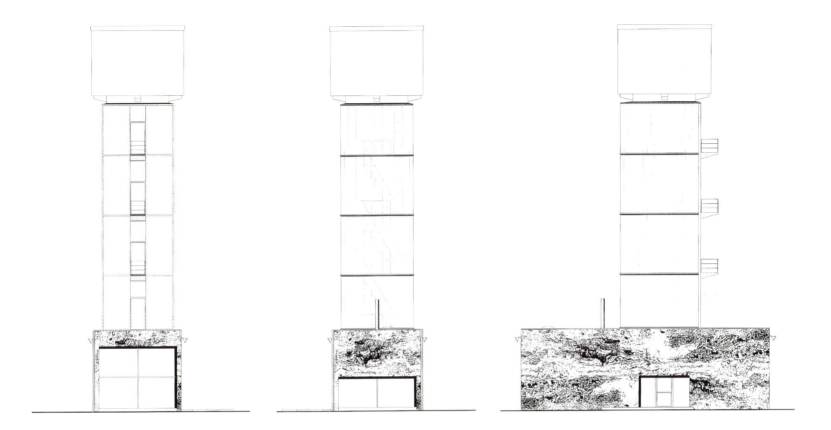

From the front, this old water tower has a very similar appearance to that of the original building. At first sight, the glass and the galvanized metal seem to be the only incorporations to the structure.

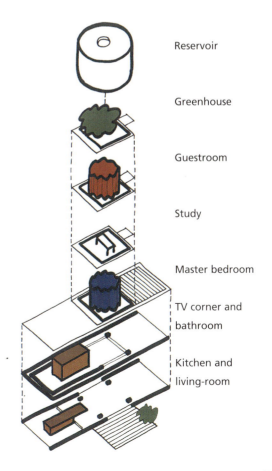

Reservoir

Greenhouse

Guestroom

Study

Master bedroom

TV corner and bathroom

Kitchen and living-room

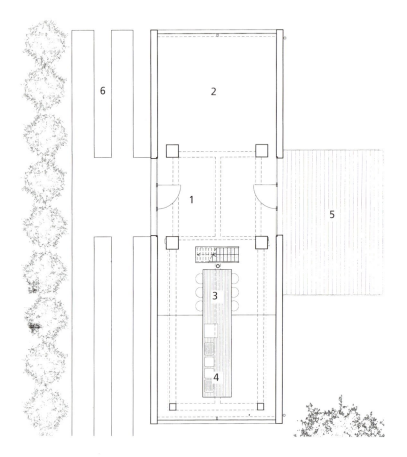
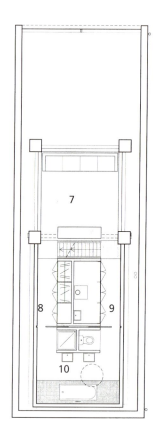

Floor plans

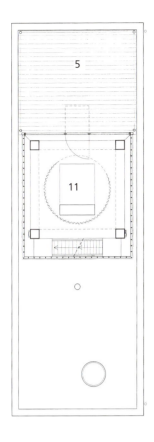
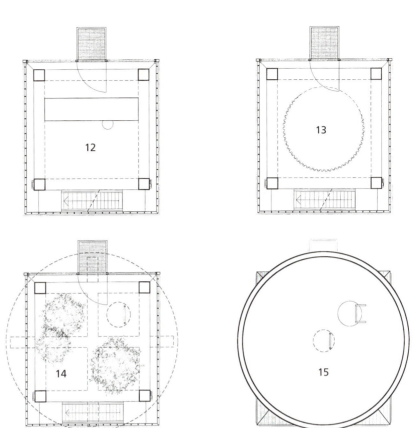

1. Entrance
2. Living-room
3. Dining
4. Kitchen
5. Terrace
6. Garage
7. TV-corner
8. Dressing
9. Storage
10. Bathroom
11. Bedroom
12. Study
13. Guestroom
14. Winter garden
15. Watertank

The construction of a larger volume on the first two floors, in which all the common areas and services are housed, breaks the spatial limitation of the rest of the floors and is the most striking feature of the tower.

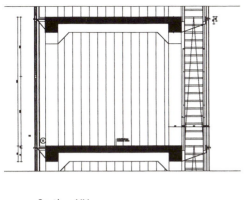

Section XX

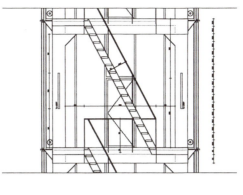

Section YY

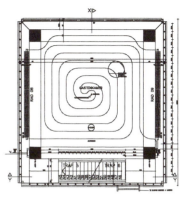

Type floor plan

Section AA   Section BB

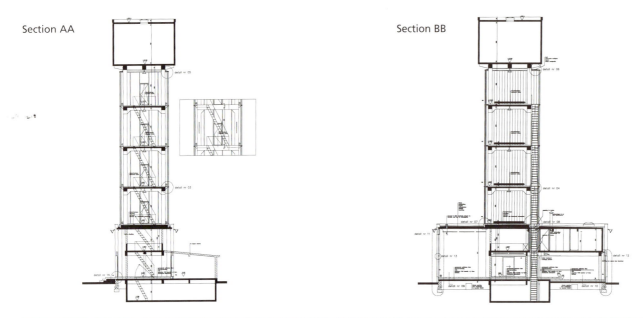

Eduardo Souto de Moura
Casa Baiâo

Baiâo, Portugal

For the Baiâo House the request of the client was to build a small residence for the weekends by restoring the old ruins of a previous building. The basic line of the project was to highlight and consolidate the remains of the old building, maintaining them as a walled garden, and to build the house completely separate.

The work began with the demolition of the supporting main wall and with the excavation of the plot to situate the house. The house itself is a block of cement sunken into the land but open towards the River Douro. The program required a "Portuguese house", respecting the beauty of the landscape. In this case, the integration was achieved by the fact that the dwelling is very concealed, practically buried in the surroundings.

Despite the limited budget, it was possible to use materials from several points of Europe: French aluminum profiles, Swiss building materials, Belgian guttering, Spanish sanitary appliances and Italian marbles and lamps, all without forgetting the local materials: some pieces from the demolitions in Barredo, rubblework from Leira and elements of woodwork from Paredes. A combination and union of elements from all over the EU come together in this small holiday residence.

Photographs: Luis Ferreira Alves

Construction detail

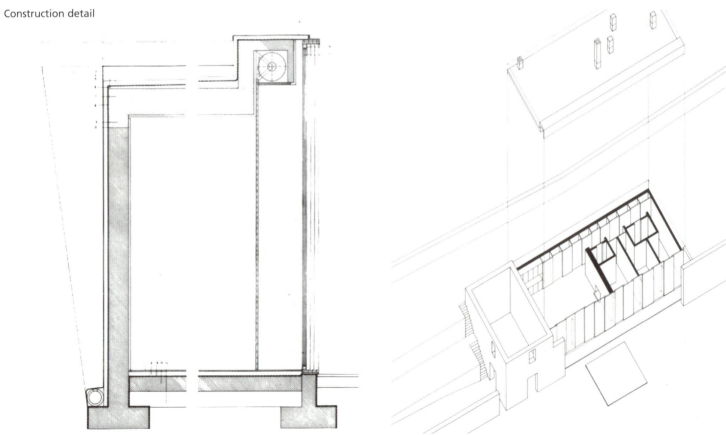

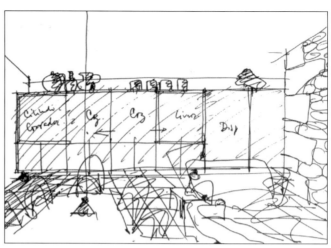
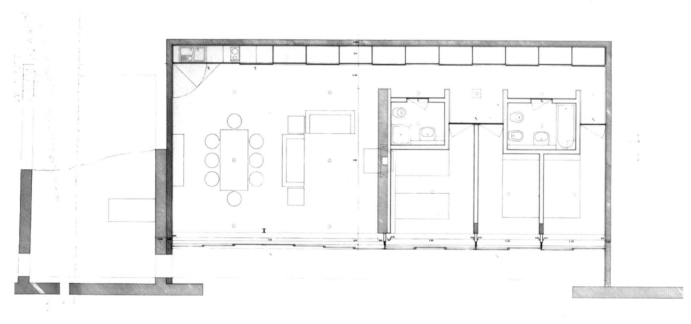
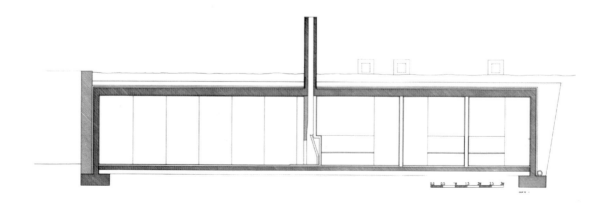

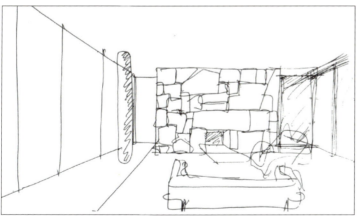 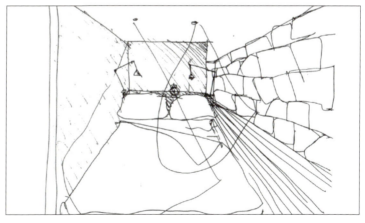

A stone wall belonging to the old ruins separates the area of the living-dining room and kitchen from the area of bedrooms and toilets. These two environments, which enjoy direct views of the garden through sliding glass doors, are communicated longitudinally by a rear corridor lined with cupboards concealed behind sliding wooden doors.

Niall McLaughlin
Northamptonshire Shack

Northamptonshire, UK

This dwelling is located on agricultural land that was used as a reconnaissance base by the allied forces during the Second World War. The building was constructed manually, without any working drawings and in conjunction with a landscape scheme, so in its development the modifications were open to all those involved.

The client, a photographer specialized in insects and nature with back lighting and special effects, wanted a house that also served as a setting for his work. He therefore decided to regenerate an abandoned pond that was lost between a labyrinth of brambles and bushes. After the water had been filtered and oxygenated with plants, the brambles and bushes had been cleared away and the water had been populated with fish, the pond recovered its life and could attract the dragonflies and other animals that would be used as models for the photographer.

The form and the materials of the building were conceived with the intention of capturing and storing several types of light. Some external spaces, such as the south area facing the pond, are used as rooms in which objects could be placed for photographing under the required conditions. A long arm was also built over the pond to photograph insects on the surface with the water as a background. To take advantage of the geographical situation of this dwelling, the architect incorporated a sauna, a bedroom and a belvedere with views over the aquatic landscape and the surrounding grasslands.

The building combines wood, masonry, metal cladding and other elements, and a glass-fiber wing whose extended staircases of polycarbonate and perforated metal emerge from the water. Due to the curious external appearance, the access to the dwelling is like the entrance to a hidden cave.

The main elements of the structure are the numerous "wing" elements that crawl over the rear part of the building, the skylight that runs along the longitudinal axis, and a complex overhanging roof supported by fine metal angles laid out in a fan-shape that bend with the force of the strong wind that blows in this area.

Photographs: Nicholas Kane

Site plan

The effects of light on the exterior are supplemented inside the dwelling by means of the incorporation of polycarbonate deflectors on the roof, just above the skylight. These are secured by fine rods and deviate the rays of light creating a pleasant illumination.

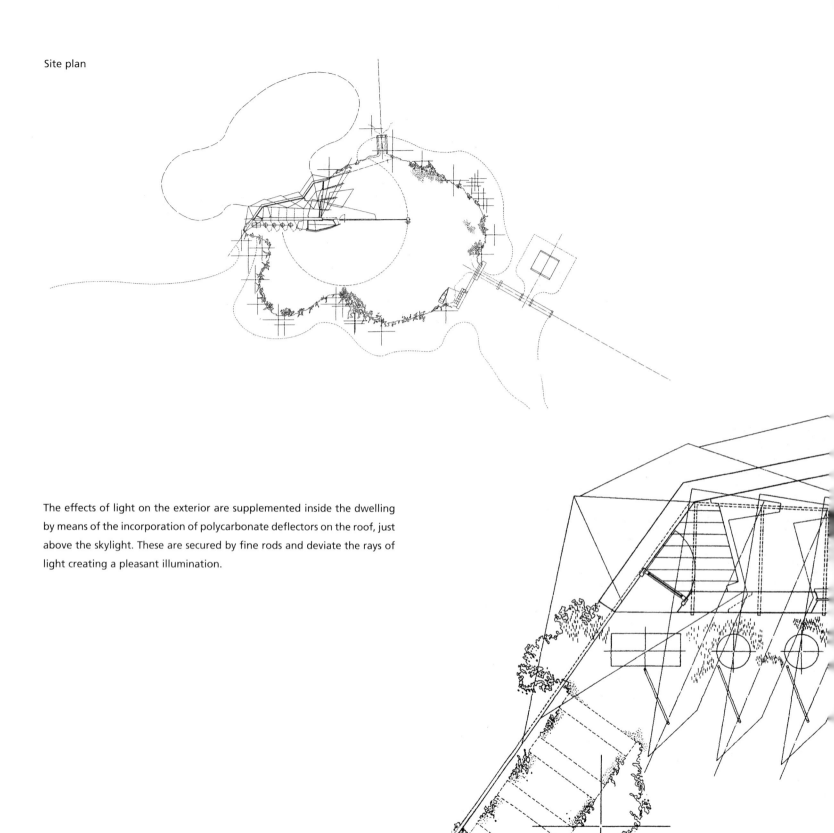

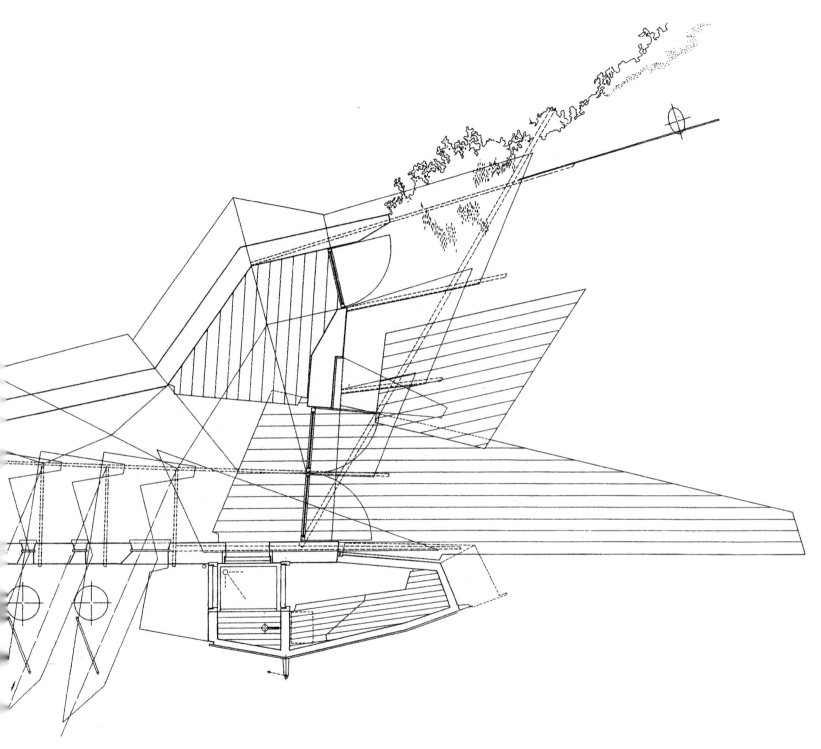

Floor plan

Arnaud Goujon Architecte DPLG
Transformed penthouse

Paris, France

In the heart of Paris, the architect Arnaud Goujon transformed an old greenhouse located at the top of a block of flats into a small and comfortable refuge with a terrace and unique views. Conceived as an extension of the loft apartment, this volume would soon become the favorite room of this home.

It is a scheme in which the initial volume was respected and a new wooden frame was superimposed on the steel structure. On the exterior, the shingle boards are made of red Canadian cedar, while the interior walls are lined with moabi panels.

The main task for the architect in this rehabilitation – apart from the technical problems – consisted of designing and organizing the different spaces of the apartment, and resolving the problems of execution and assembly of the different materials.

The absence of exposed fittings on the wall panels of the interior helps to enlarge and unify the volume of the main room, which opens on both sides onto a terrace of 50 m^2 covered with a jatoba wood deck and offering spectacular views of the urban landscape.

The interior of this unusual dwelling is composed only of a living room with an open integrated kitchen, in which a chimney is framed between two shelves, and a small bedroom with its bathroom. This room enjoys the benefit of two sources of natural light that illuminate this more private area: a small window in the back wall and a skylight located over the bed. The floor of the interior is made of chestnut parquet covered with white polyurethane paint that reduces the color saturation and brings freshness to the dwelling.

The wood, chosen for its plastic and structural qualities, is used as a double skin: soft and beautiful in the interior and rough and sturdy on the exterior. Thus, although this organic material is set against the urban nature of an environment in which steel is the main component, its form fits well into the geometric pattern of the building.

Photographs: Joel Cariou

The terrace surrounding this apartment is one of its fundamental elements. The panoramic views of Paris are an additional feature that enhances the architectural work.

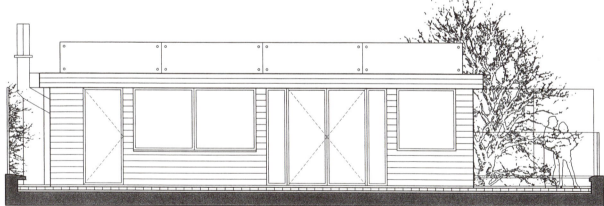

East elevation

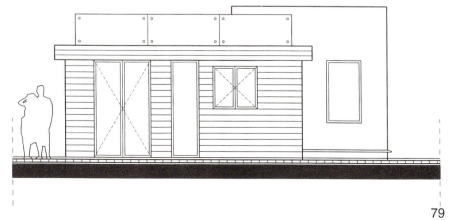

North elevation

Floor plan

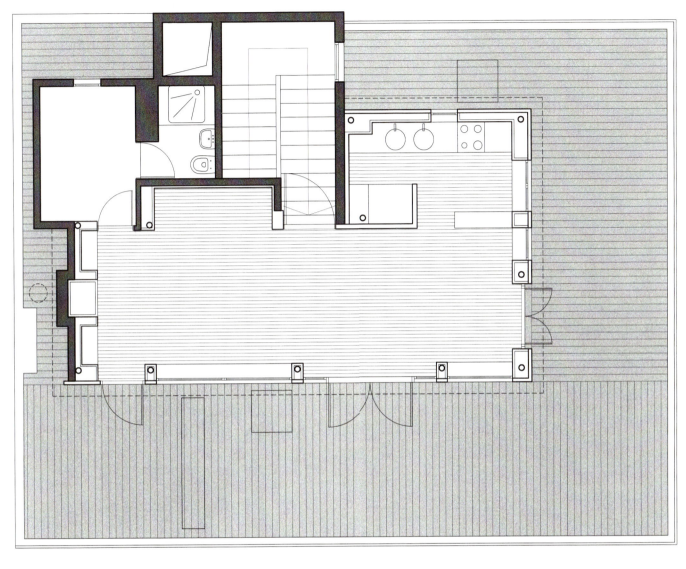

Vertical section of wood wall   Vertical section of window

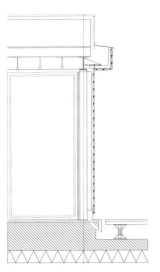

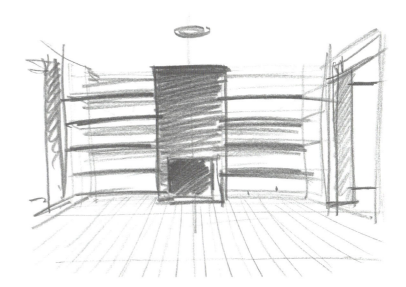

Gray Organschi
Tennis House

Connecticut, USA

Tennis House forms part of a large forest area in the north-west of the state of Connecticut. The building is located at the end of a small valley, on a site that was formerly a gravel pit; but which now, after the discovery of an underground spring, is occupied by a pond surrounded by wild grasslands. In the design of this property the architects aimed to negotiate the relationship between the qualities of the site and the creation of a garden, in which a tennis court is the main feature.

Because the lands at the end of the valley were protected by recent environmental regulations, the habitable spaces of the building had to comply with the legal limits. However, the clients presented an ambitious scheme that included two dressing rooms, a bathroom, service rooms, a kitchen with utility room, a pantry, a bedroom with bunks and a living room at the level of the tennis court. The court has retaining walls made of concrete blocks on three of its sides, leaving the side furthest from the dwelling open, with views of the pond. Clover and vetch were planted up to the edges of these walls, giving lightness to elements that tend to offer a very solid appearance. The tennis court looks as if it had been cut cleanly out of the land, and is aligned at the same level as the surface of the pond. Overlooking the court at its south end, the dwelling is embedded into the hillside. The concrete retaining wall that forms the building's back elevation is transformed along its length to create an exterior shower, a sink counter for the bathroom, a storage wall containing the kitchenette and laundry, a rear staircase, an interior fireplace and exterior grill, and ultimately a catch basin for the roof's rainwater runoff.

Along the facade facing the tennis court, ten columns and a "box" of cypress wood containing the dressing rooms and the indoor shower support the roof, which is trapezoidal and has a low corner from which the rainwater can drain off. This roof was covered with vegetation, forming a pure plane of grass that is only interrupted by the chimney and a skylight that illuminates the dressing rooms.

Photographs: Edward Hueber

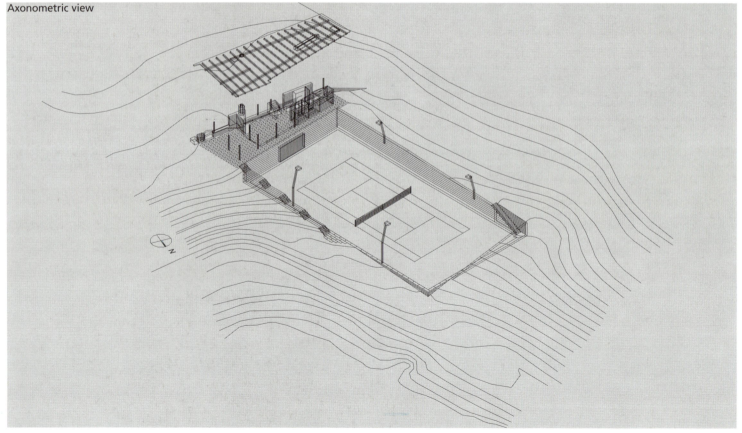
Axonometric view

The dwelling is articulated around the tennis court and the pond, so from the main living areas, such as the living room and the terrace on the upper floor, one can enjoy the views or watch a tennis match.

de Architectengroep (Dick van Gameren & Bjarne Mastenbroek)
Apartments in a sewage plant

Amsterdam, The Netherlands

In the garden city of Amsterdam-West, the concrete reservoir tanks of a former sewage plant have been converted into a housing project. Although the original master plan called for seven circular, urban villas on an open green strip between two neighborhoods, it was deemed much more interesting to juxtapose the site's raw, industrial elements with new dwellings, as opposed to relying on a blank slate to create a project with only a formal resemblance to the original elements.

The experiment of converting slurry tanks and pre-treatment facilities into housing and services for a new neighborhood offered the chance to give a unique signature to the development, something often lacking in new housing developments.

Three of the existing concrete drums were used. One was made into storage facilities for the adjacent dwellings; another was used as a gray water collection tank with an overflow leading to a nearby lake; and the third was converted into a small apartment building. 30% of this last drum has been cut away in order to bring natural light into the apartments. The existing circular wall now serves as a screen between the new apartments and their immediate exterior surroundings. Each floor contains a three-room apartment and a small studio.

Since the penthouse on top sits above the top of the wall of the concrete drum, it enjoys privileged 360-degree views of Amsterdam-West, the park and the lake. In contrast to this wide view, total privacy is achieved in the central living room by the absence of windows; instead, natural light filters through a skylight. All the other rooms, including a second living room, are situated along the perimeter. Movement through the building and apartments constantly shifts from completely introverted (the drum itself and the living room) to extroverted (all the other rooms, kitchen and terraces).

Photographs: Nicholas Kane

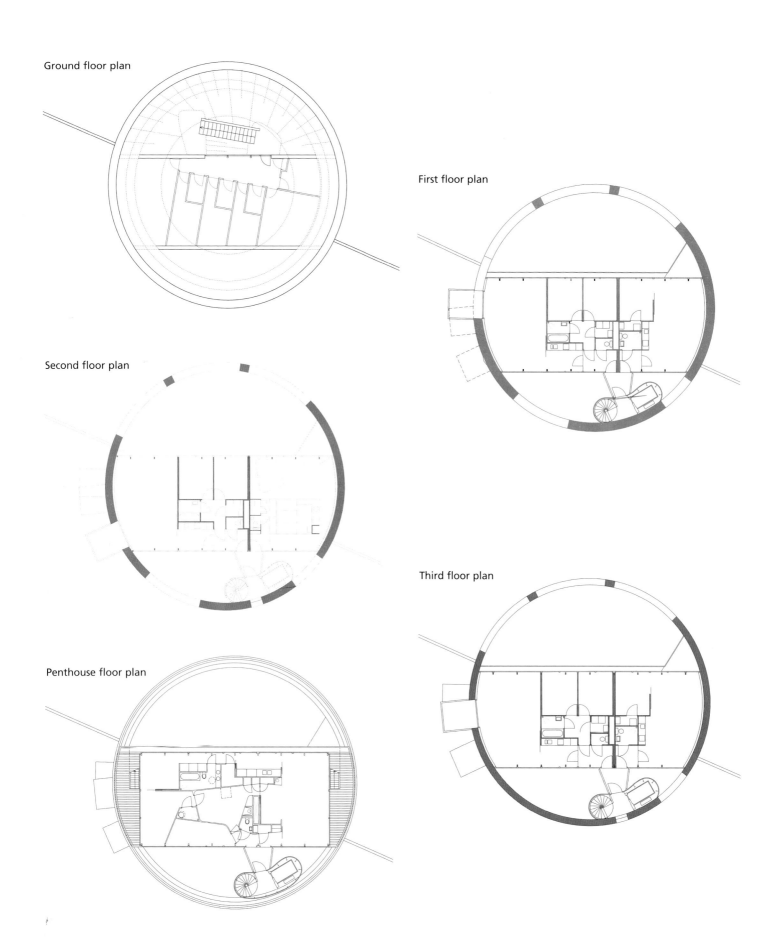

Of the three converted concrete drums, the one containing the dwellings has had 30% of its existing walls removed in order to bring natural light into the facade-side of the apartments and along the back, where each floor has a protruding balcony.

Section

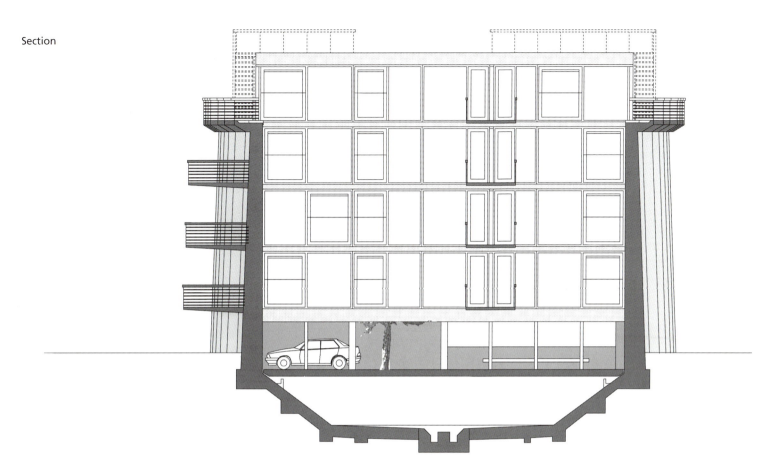

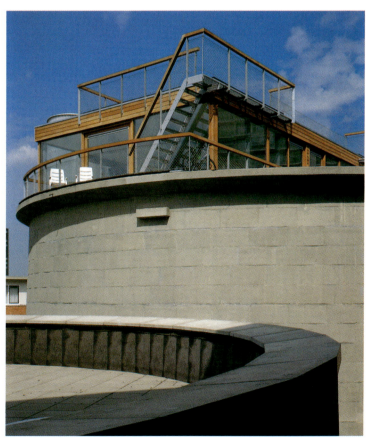

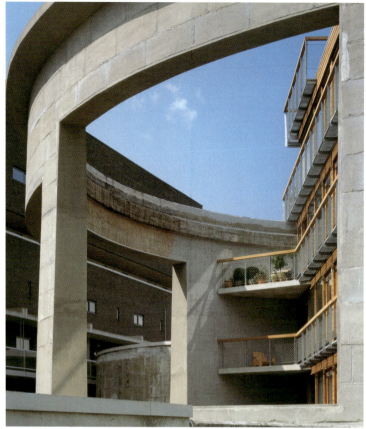

1. Balcony
2. Garden
3. Living-room
4. Utility room
5. Tatami room
6. Bathroom
7. Entrance
8. Studio

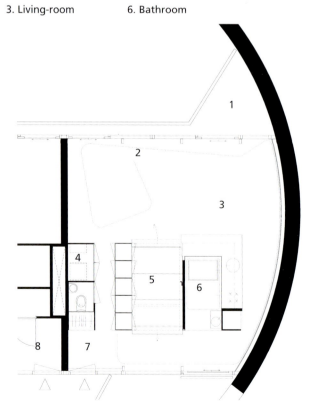

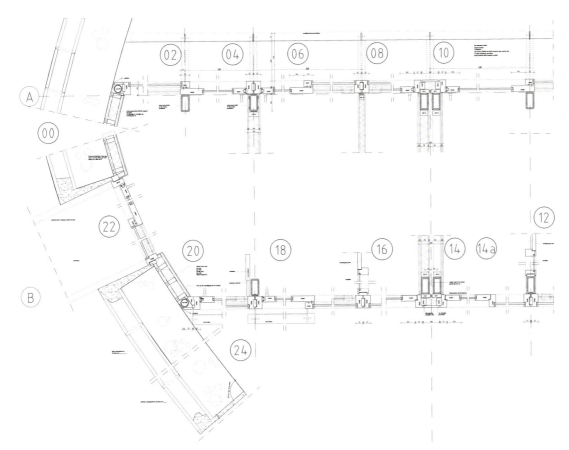

As seen on the opposite page, the building is accessed via a translucent, cylindrical shaft housing the elevator and stair. This volume stands independent of the building, yet within the concrete drum.

Sean Godsell
Carter / Tucker House

Breamlea, Australia

A three level, three bedroom, 12m X 6m box was embedded into the side of a sand dune. The lower ground floor is for guests and the single space can be divided by a sliding wall into two rooms if so required. Similarly the single space on the middle level can also be divided to separate the owner's bedroom from a small sitting area. The top floor is for living and eating and takes advantage of views across a rural landscape.

In traditional Chinese architecture the aisle is a fluid outer building which is continuous around the perimeter of the inner building. In traditional Japanese architecture the aisle (*gejin*) is not continuous when added to a structure, but is fluid space when an inner building is partitioned (*hedate*) to cause an aisle to be formed.

The traditional outback Australian homestead is also surrounded by fluid space (the verandah) which is sometimes partly enclosed with flywire or glass to form an indoor/outdoor space (sunroom). Where in cooler climates the roof of the aisle provides shelter from snow and rain, in the outback the verandah helps shade the vertical surfaces of the building from direct solar radiation. The Carter/Tucker house is primarily an investigation of the verandah/aisle and its potential as an iconic element common between eastern and western architecture.

The verandah exists in this house in an abstracted form. On all three levels the outer (timber screen) skin of the building tilts open and forms a verandah on the perimeter of the building. This component allows the fluidity of the aisle space to transfer itself across the façade of the building.

On the middle level, the bedroom then becomes the verandah while the corridor, formed by the insertion of a service core, becomes the inner room. Depending on the time of the year the verandah can then be enclosed with sliding flyscreens to become a sunroom, or left open.

The bedroom space can then be further modified by the operation of the *hedate* wall which when drawn across the bedroom forms an inner building within the aisle. The idea of fluid space is further emphasized by the service core being kept free from both ends of the building so that movement through the floor is continuous - no steps have to be retraced.

Photographs: Earl Carter ·

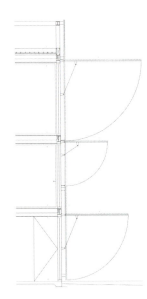

The verandah exists in this house in an abstracted form. Elements of the object exist throughout the building while its traditional form is not immediately evident. On all three levels the outer, timber-screen skin of the building tilts open to create a verandah on the perimeter of the building. The horizontal plane of the ceiling is thus extended beyond the building line.

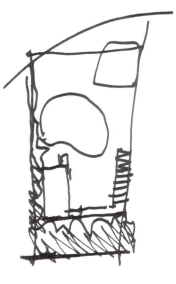

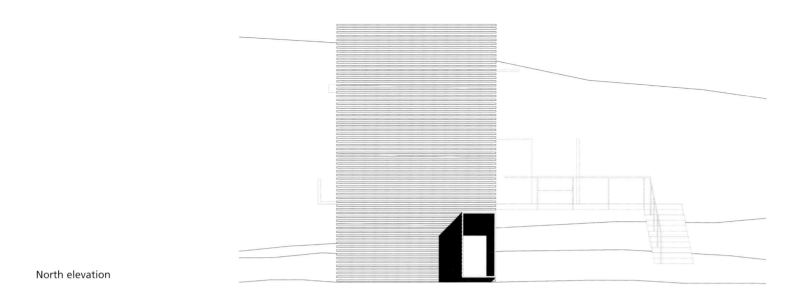

North elevation

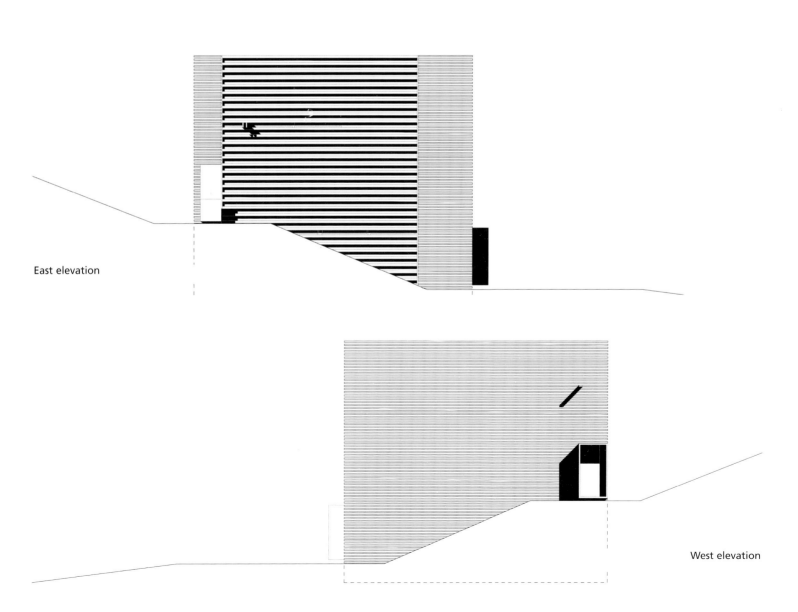

East elevation

West elevation

107

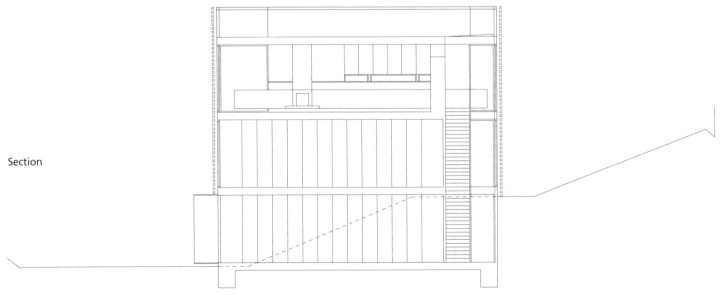

Section

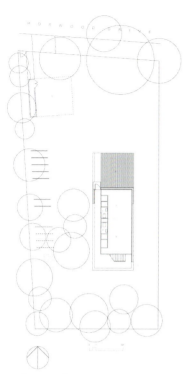

Basement

The façades are veiled with a system of adjustable louvers which blur the edges of the building and constantly modify its appearance depending upon the position of the viewer. Light enters or is prevented from entering the building in a constantly changing way.

Basement plan

Ground floor plan

First floor plan

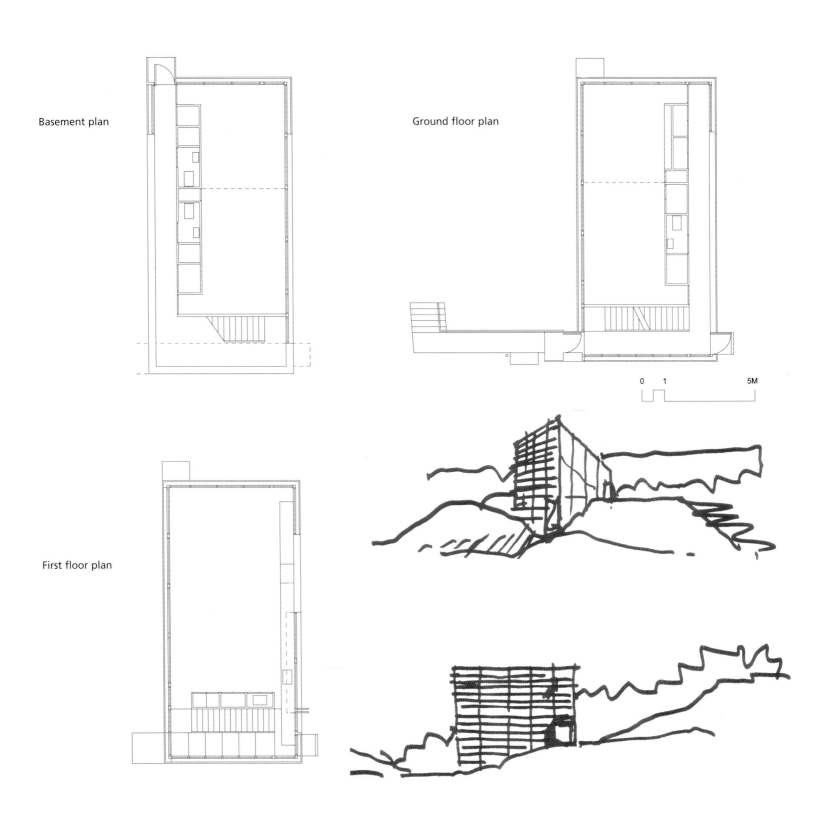

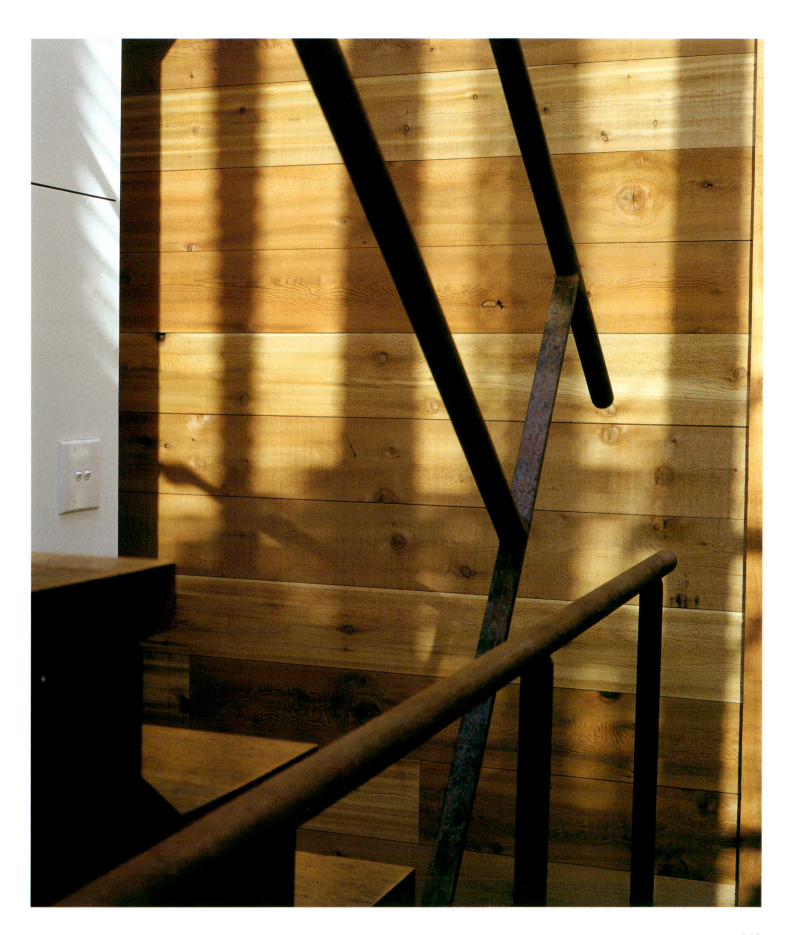

Satoshi Okada Architects
Villa Man-Bow

Atami, Japan

This project is a villa located in the mountains of Atami, a famous spa resort on the Pacific Ocean, about 100 km west of Tokyo. The plot is on a steep and rocky mountain ridge, with a grade of approximately 70 degrees, facing north to splendid views of the ocean beyond the valley down below. It is some 9 meters above the front street, which, in general, makes for difficult building conditions. To make matters worse, the area is noted for strong winds, high humidity and dense fogs, as well as frequent earthquakes. In particular, the salty gales blowing up through the narrow valley from the ocean represent the greatest danger to buildings in the vicinity. The strength of these furious winds has been known to knock down walls or blow off roofs during each typhoon season.

The client wanted to build a villa which would also function as a guesthouse for weekend parties in the country. The conditions that had to be addressed were: 1) dealing with the humidity of the site; 2) ensuring the splendid view of the ocean above the tree-tops; 3) mitigating the strong winds.

In lifting the building piloti-style above the ground, the architect immediately solved some of the site's more salient problems: the building is no longer obliged to conform to the steep grade of the land, humidity emanating from the ground does not enter the house and clearer views above the tree-tops are gained.

The villa is composed of two volumes; one is an ellipsoidal sphere housing most of the home's general functions, the other is a rectangular parallelepiped solely for sleeping. Each volume is supported by 6 columns of 30 cm of diameter, on a 3.6 m grid formation. As protection against the wind, the sphere faces the valley in an aerodynamic manner, while the rectangle is shielded by thick tree cover. In both, the main skeleton is steel, and the ellipsoidal cage is shaped by laminated timbers.

The exterior of the ellipsoid is entirely clad in copper plates (t=0.35 mm), a technique for which the project is indebted to the traditional technique of shrine carpenters in Japan. The greenish patina which will accrue over time will serve as protection against the corrosion caused by the high salt content of the seaside air.

As per the client's request, interior surfaces are all painted white. In the sphere particularly, one can experience a certain endless space through voids, as well as one's own unreliable senses for understanding space without corners. This game of perception between architectural space and the human body provides the extraordinary aspect sought by the clients.

Photographs: Hiroyuki Hirai

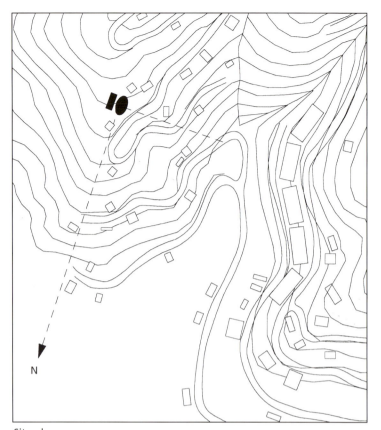
Site plan

The site is on a steep, rocky mountain ridge, with a gradient of approximately 70 degrees, and faces north to enjoy a splendid view of the ocean beyond the valley.
The villa is composed of two volumes; one is an ellipsoidal sphere for living, the other is a rectangular parallelepiped solely for sleeping.

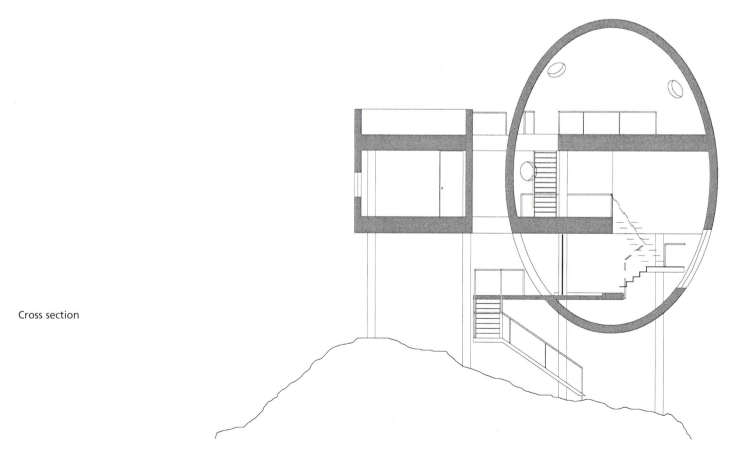
Cross section

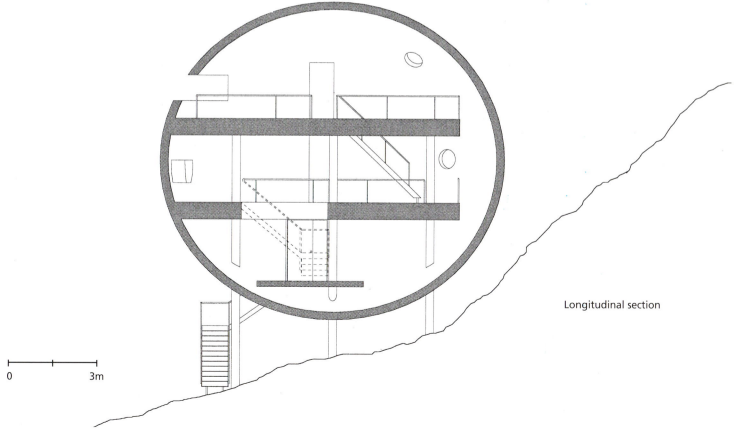

Longitudinal section

0 3m

Entrance floor plan

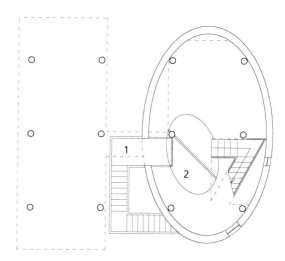

1. Entrance porch 2. Entrance 3. Hall 4. Gallery 5. Anteroom 6. Bedroom

First floor plan

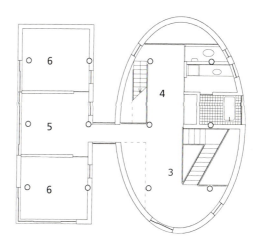

The exterior of the sphere is entirely clad in copper plates, for which the project is indebted to the traditional techniques of shrine carpenters in Japan. The greenish patina which will accrue over time will serve as protection against the corrosion caused by the high salt content of the seaside air.

Second floor plan

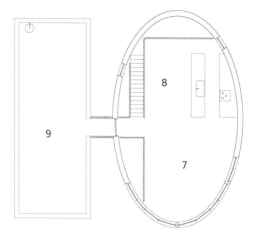

7. Living room
8. Dining room
9. Roof terrace

As per the client's request, interior surfaces are all painted white. In the sphere particularly, one can experience a certain endless space through voids, as well as one's own unreliable senses for understanding space without corners. This game of perception between architectural space and the human body provides the extraordinary aspect sought by the clients.

José Gigante
Wind Mill Conversion

Vilar de Mouros / Caminha, Portugal

In the grounds of a recovered house in northern Portugal, an old abandoned windmill waited its turn to be useful again. In the course of time the idea finally arose of transforming this peculiar building into a small auxiliary dwelling belonging to the main house, giving it its own life and thus creating a completely inhabitable and independent space that could be used as a place of rest. For José Gigante, the presence of the mill was so strong that any major intervention would have minimized its charm.

Therefore, without touching any of the thick granite walls, an unusual copper roof with a very gentle slope was added. The intention was to respect the memory of the place as far as possible, so the inspiration for the transformation began naturally from the inside towards the outside. The layout and organization of the small space, with only eight square meters per floor, was not easy. Thanks to the choice of wood as the main building material, a welcoming atmosphere enhanced by the curved walls and the few openings was achieved. On the lower floor, an impressive rock acts as an entrance step. On this level it was attempted to achieve a minimum space in which it was possible to carry out different activities. It houses a bathroom and a living room, with the possibility of transforming a small sofa into a curious bed: it is conceived as a case that contains all the necessary pieces for assembling the bed. On the upper floor, the furnishings are limited to a cupboard and a table/bed that is extended to the window.

The only openings are those that already existed in the mill and they have been left as they were conceived, with their natural capacity to reveal the exterior and to illuminate a space in which the contrasts between the materials cannot be ignored. The typology of this building was crucial to the restorations to which it has been subjected, and shows why the interior space is so important in this scheme. The thick circular walls occupy more space than the interior of the mill, but they hug the whole room and provide a welcoming and unconventional sensation that give this building a new and innovative perspective.

Photographs: Luís Ferreira Alves

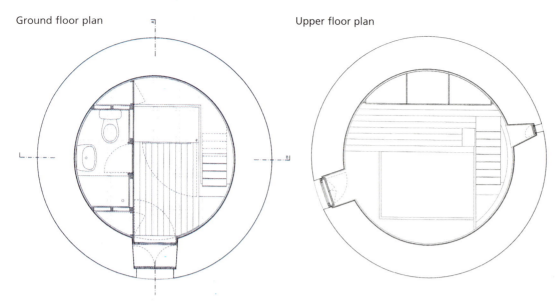

Ground floor plan

Upper floor plan

To solve the problem of the lack of space, a system was devised in which a bed is hidden at the foot of the staircase.

Marin-Trottin (Péripheriqués Architectes)
MR House

Pompone, France

Stretched along a strip of marshy land in the Seine and Marne region, this metal-frame house seems to form part of the landscape. The dwelling slopes with the 15% drop in land level and is camouflaged by greenery, while the painted panels of the façade blend with the garden. Huge windows frame the lower and upper gardens, thus highlighting the relationship between interior and exterior. As a final touch, small shutters allow the fresh scent of the garden to waft into the home.

The tight, narrow plot of 17 meters in length gave rise to an elongated design which has the advantage of reducing the building's visual impact on the garden. By the same token, this strip-form creates an historical link with the farming activity that used to take place on the site. The rooms unfold along the slope, from the living room to the bedroom. Both public and private spaces are conceived as half-stories so as to be in close contact with the garden at all times.

Intended as a follow-up to design work undertaken for the "36 Proposals for a Home" project, this scheme illustrates the designers' ambition to make an architect-designed house for basically the same price as a prefab home, while ensuring that it meshes subtly with its surroundings.

Photographs: H. Abadie

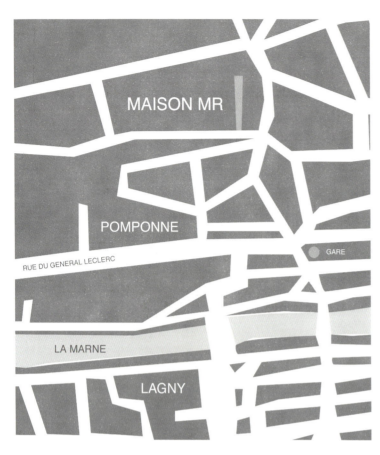

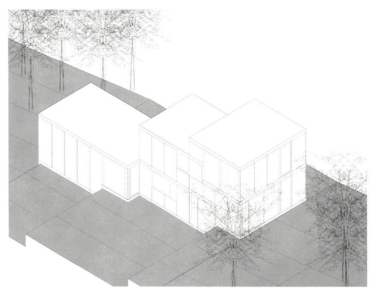

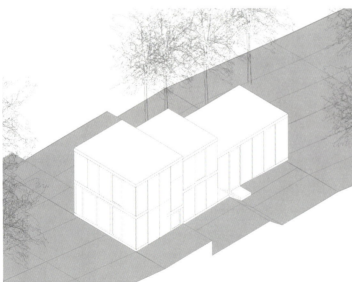

The sequence on the opposite page illustrates the inspiration behind the design of the façades. The colored panels were based on a pixilated abstraction of a garden and represent the natural variations in color tone and intensity of light.

façade ouest

Longitudinal section

The sketches of the four façades illustrate how the designers made every effort to adapt the design scheme to the natural lay of the land, thus adding a great deal of variation in an otherwise uniform, rectangular ground plan.

façade est

façade sud

façade nord

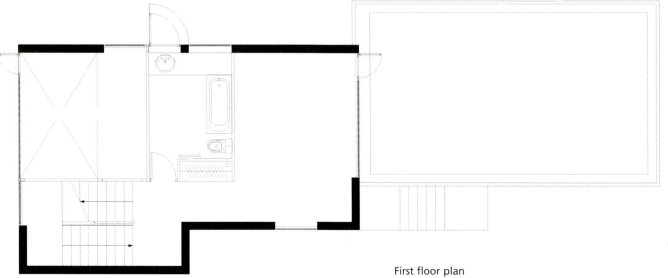

First floor plan

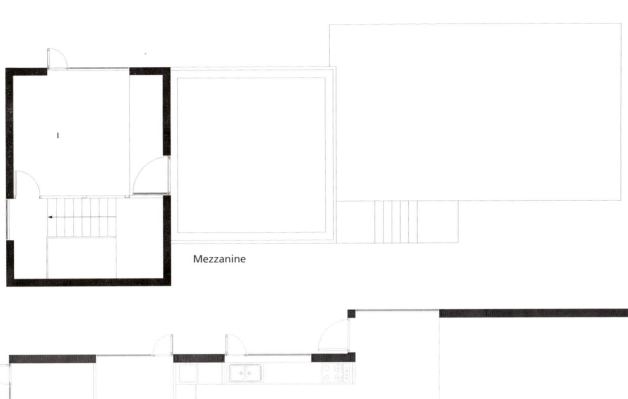

Mezzanine

Ground floor plan

139

The rooms unfold along the slope, from the living room to the bedroom. Both public and private spaces are conceived as half-stories so as to be in close contact with the garden at all times.

Philip Gumuchdjian
D.P. Think Tank / Boathouse

Skibbereen, County Cork, Ireland

Partially overhanging the River Ilen in west Ireland, the building was conceived as a retreat for a well known film producer. The architecture reflects a wide range of references: boathouse structures, barns, cow sheds, chalets, and a European perspective on Japanese pavilions. The building resolves these references into a simple expression of frame, roof and screens.

The dominant element of the design is the overhanging roof structure, which provides physical and psychological protection from the considerable annual rainfall.

A clear hierarchy of architectural elements (roof, structure, screens and glazing) was crucial to creating its legibility as an apparently enclosed "found" structure — a simple and timeless object. Transparency and perforated screens were deployed to keep the building open to the elements but also frame views and suggest enclosure and protection.

The materials of the structure are selected to juxtapose "stable" elements such as glass and stainless steel against the highly "changeable" and weathering materials of the cedar roof planks, slats and decks and the iroko frame. Set against the vivid colors and reflections of the site — green fields, blue/silver river, dramatic blues and greys of the sky— the silver of the building permanently changes color as roof and structural frame are wettened during rainshowers and bleached by the sun.

Photographs: W. Hutchmacher / ARTUR

Longitudinal section

Site plan

Side elevation

Floor plan

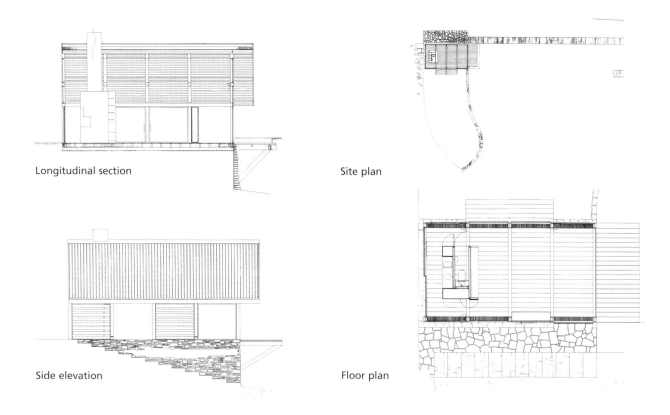

A long pier extends the house onto the river, creating a space for escape and a perspective from which the interior of this small dwelling can be appreciated.

Takao Shiotsuka
Shigemi House

Oita, Japan

Various factors and considerations came into play when determining the final form that this house would take. Its unusual shape was developed for specific reasons.

First was the wish to protect the façades, which are clad in wooden boards, from the rain. Another was to create the feeling of a spacious interior without actually increasing the ground space available. Additionally, continuity with the landscape was a goal. The access road slopes up toward the house, the embankment falls away on one side and rises on the other. So instead of standardized 90° angles, the architects instead opted for sloped façades.

The clients run a timber company and wished to fill the home, inside and out, with their company's product. Their original suggestion was to create wide eaves as a necessity for protecting the fine wood of the façades from the elements.

Instead, the architects proposed tilting the perimeter walls outward, thus creating a unified shape that fulfilled the function of eaves. This exterior treatment has the additional advantage of broadening perspectives within the home as well. The total area of the ceiling is 130 m^2, while that of the floor space is 100 m^2.

Photographs: Kaori Ichikawa

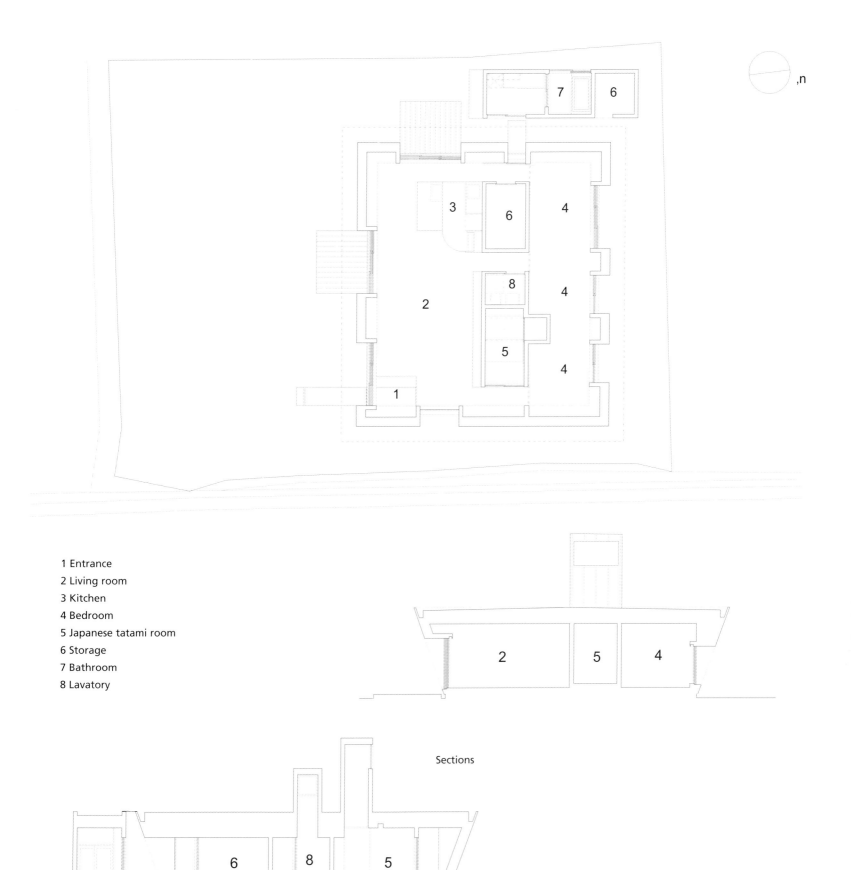

1 Entrance
2 Living room
3 Kitchen
4 Bedroom
5 Japanese tatami room
6 Storage
7 Bathroom
8 Lavatory

Sections

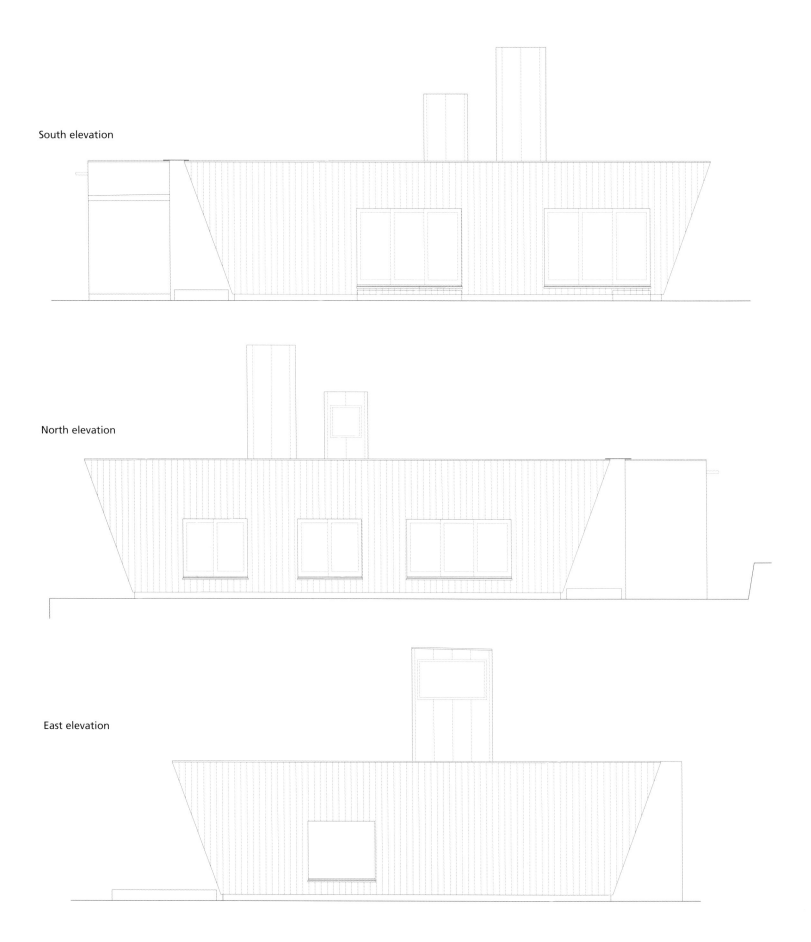

South elevation

North elevation

East elevation

West elevation

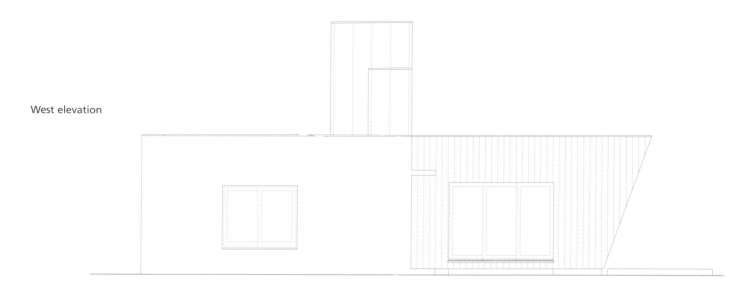

157

Daniele Marques & Bruno Zurkirchen
Haus Kraan Lang

Emmenbrücke, Switzerland

The plot for which the single-family dwelling was to be designed is located in an area with a heterogeneous planning situation, a zone of agglomeration in which the urban fabric gives way to the countryside. There are buildings with different uses in the immediate surroundings: farm buildings, cubic zigzag apartment blocks built in the sixties, and in the immediate vicinity a concrete single-family dwelling.

The aim of the architectural design was to respond to the planning regulations by means of two floors consisting of an ephemeral container in opposition to the solid constructions.

Both the ground floor containing the living area and the upper floor containing the bedrooms are south facing. The living area opens onto a covered veranda that is slightly lower than the top of the sliding windows, thus making full use of natural light. The north side is closed in response to the railway line located nearby.

The position of the container, in exact relation to the neighboring concrete single-family dwelling, is intended to define an exterior space belonging to both houses. The single-family dwelling is prefabricated, the constructional system being based on large panels for light constructions and pillars resting on a pedestal in the basement. It is covered with untreated trapezoidal aluminum sheet. This aluminum cladding was used for all the exterior surfaces, including the roof. The remaining wooden constructional elements were left untreated, except for a wax coating.

Photographs: Daniel Mayer

Site plan

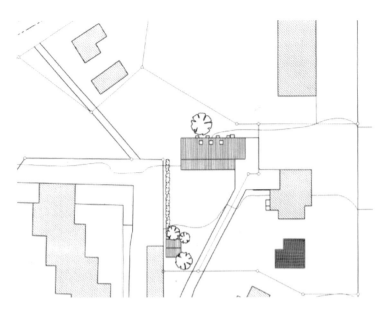

A study of the environment of the project enables us to define the spatial logic of the building. The model shows the desire of the architects to distinguish them from the progressive development of this formerly rural area, which is now, a total planning chaos. The site plan shows how the articulation with the neighboring concrete house manages to create a more formalized exterior space.

The large aluminum panels that recall industrial containers create an unexpected and subversive effect in the context and give nobility to the house despite their low cost and ephemeral appearance.

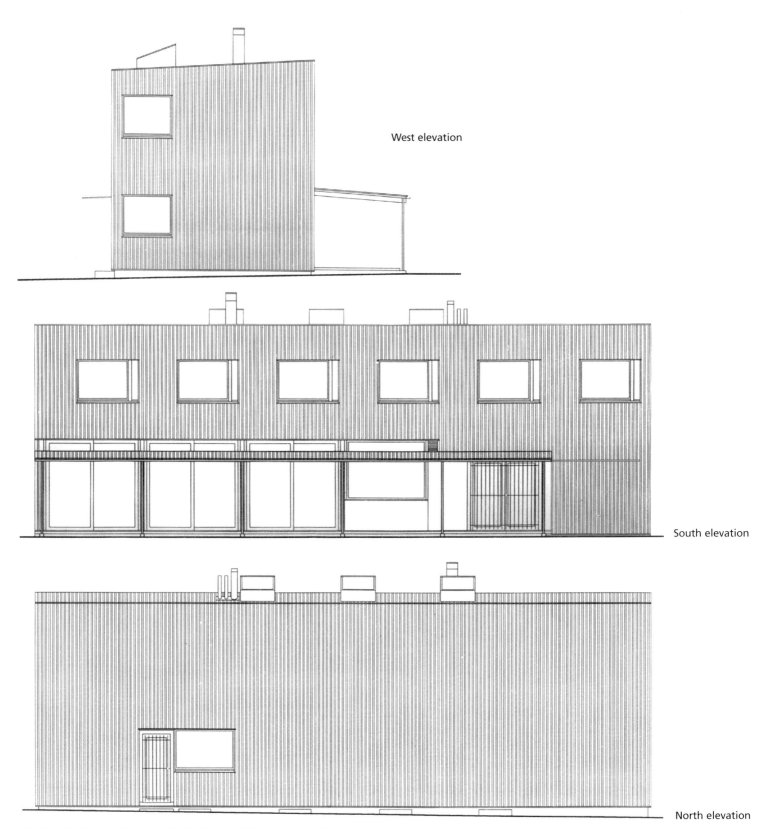

North side: the facade is practically blind, which responds to the nearby railway line, provides privacy from the large adjoining apartment blocks and increases the thermal comfort of the house.

167

First floor plan

Ground floor plan

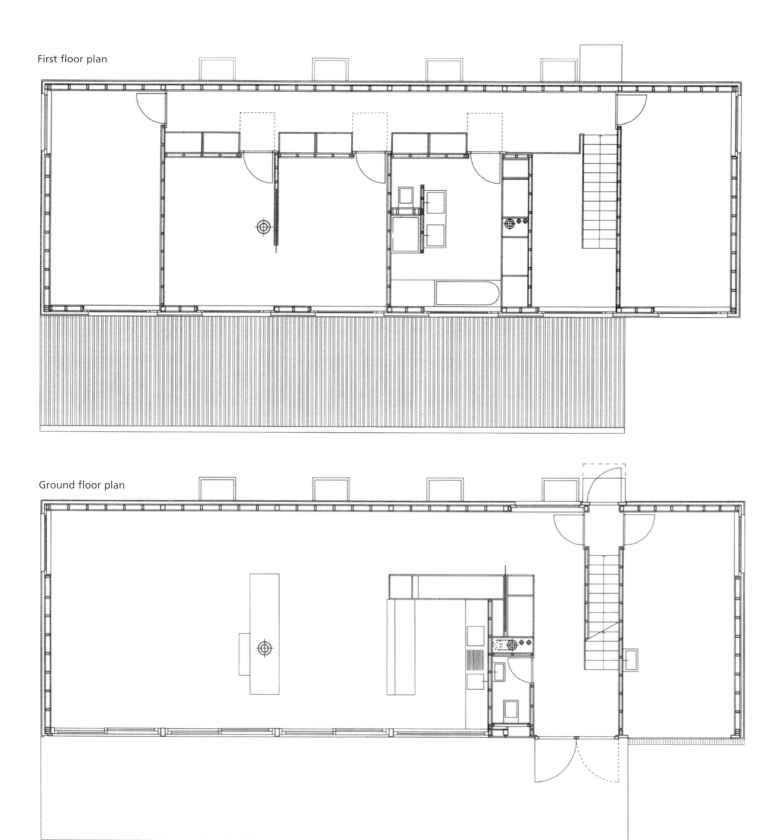

The large rectangle of the container is regulated with great simplicity and rationality by a grid in six equal divisions that correspond to the interior partition walls and the pillars of the portico on the south facade. The width of the portico preserves certain privacy on the ground floor, screening it from the overlooking apartment blocks.

Cross section

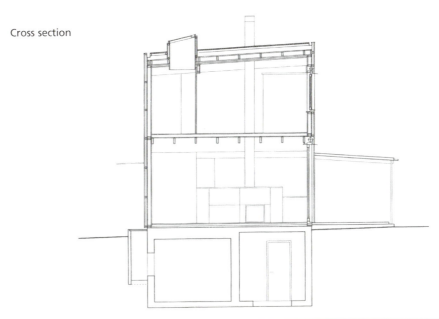

The interiors emanate certain Loosian sensitivity: great importance is given to the materials, their natural use and their visual impact. The association between the metals, the wood (untreated and waxed) and the glass, with its reflections, brilliance and transparency, provide a tone of luxury and warmth in counterpoint to the external appearance.

Shigeru Ban
Paper House

Yamanakako, Japan

Shigeru Ban has been studying the characteristics of paper as a building element since the eighties. Though there is some resistance to its use in a structural system, paper is a material that may be treated (like wood) to make it resistant to fire, water and damp. It is also easy to recycle and economic. This allowed the architect to work with this element in designs that required speed and low cost, such as the pavilions for refugees from Ruanda and the provisional buildings to house the victims of the Kobe earthquake.

In this scheme, a dwelling of 110 m^2, the structure is formed by two square horizontal planes with a side of 10 meters and paper tubes aligned in an S-shape with a height of 2.7 meters, a diameter of 280 mm and a thickness of 15 mm. These tubes support the house and defined its different functional spaces, relating them to the surrounding landscape. Ten of these tubes support the vertical loads and eighty interior tubes support the lateral loads. The circle formed by these eighty tubes defines the living room, whereas the circle formed by the square defines the bathroom of the dwelling.

The separation from the exterior is created using a glass wall that may open or close and that can also be covered by canvas curtains to provide privacy and good insulation.

The spatial continuity between the interiors and the landscape is achieved through the horizontal elements and the use of very diaphanous joinery, and through the definition of the interior spaces with the minimum number of elements, following the example of the great architects of Modernism.

The paper tubes also allow the spaces defined to maintain a very subtle relation with the surrounding spaces, allowing in the light and views between them.

Photographs: Hiroyuki Hirai

Floor plan

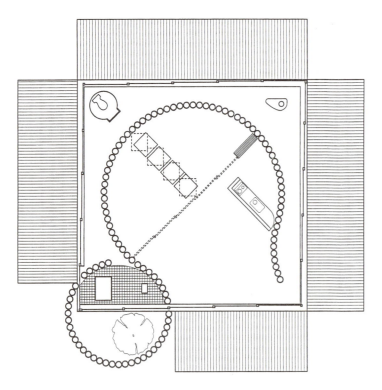

Cross-section

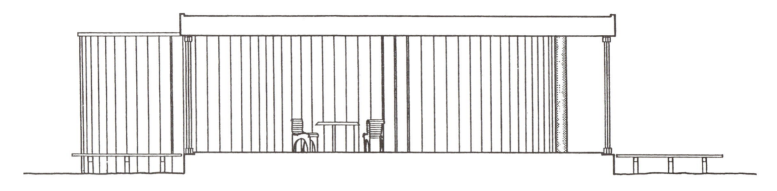

The relation between the interior and exterior spaces is a constant in the designs of Shigeru Ban. In this scheme, the enormous glazed window can be opened to leave the dwelling totally open to the exterior. To emphasize this relation even further, overhanging terraces were created to extend the floor area and bring the dwelling closer to nature.

Flemming Skude
Con Cave

Hummingen, Lolland, Denmark

Somehow this grounded house represents quite the opposite of Glenn Murcutt's credo: "Touch this earth lightly" although it could also be seen as a current exponent for the building tradition in Denmark. Nature-integrated and aerodynamic dwellings can be traced thousands of years back to the Iron Age. At that time dwellings used to be sunk about a meter into the terrain and covered by a thatched roof. Even built on hills, problems of flooding and water in heavy rain periods could occur. (In Iceland, the Faroe Islands and in Greenland this house type has survived up to our days with stones and turf on the outside and wooden panels on the inside.)

During the Viking era (ca. 750-1050 CE) solitary buildings often had a ship-like plan since carpenters from shipmaking knew well that a rectangular form acted badly against waves of the sea and forces of the wind. Because of this latter fact the Con Cave house has its maximum width and height along its middle and is crowned by a skylight at the top of the roof where its predecessors used to have an opening for letting out smoke from the fireplace. In fact the details of the ceiling in Con Cave look very shiplike from the inside.

From the outside the house recalls dolmens or cromlechs of the Bronze Era, also since the main entrance is flanked by stones in the way used for graveyards in those days. This means that from the outside this house is expected to be very cold and dark on the inside; yet quite the opposite is true.

In fact Con Cave should be understood as a wooden coffin placed above the surrounding terrain and protected sidewards by a wall of concrete blocks preventing the covering soil sides from pressing the facades towards the house. Oriented strictly on an east-west axis, the earth coverings make 3 natural terraces to the south, east and west. Technically the inside wood construction has a normal insulation of 10 centimeters and is ventilated on all sides as well as in the roofing. The outside of the wood coffin has a strong Platon membrane (normally used on external basement walls) protecting against humidity and moisture. On the top of this membrane there are two layers of turf about 12 cm thick.

By covering a "normal" wood construction by earthern slopes and grass turf, the final outcome is an overall aerodynamic form and a major improvement in natural temperature control since CON CAVE is never under 5º C during the winter. The house also has a pleasant cooler average temperature than the outside in the summer, without any artificial ventilation devices. The owner of the house in fact never wanted a hearth in the first place but has installed a few electrical stoves, just in case. The outcome of this simple house with small facades covered with copper at top (like the cladding of the skylight) requires a minimum of maintenance, a cosy dwelling and almost no heating expenses. The 'horns' over the gables to the east and the west are intended for hanging up sun-protecting sails, but so far have never been put to work.

Photographs: Flemming Skude

Site plan

Floor plan

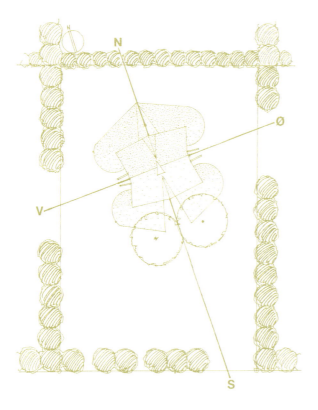
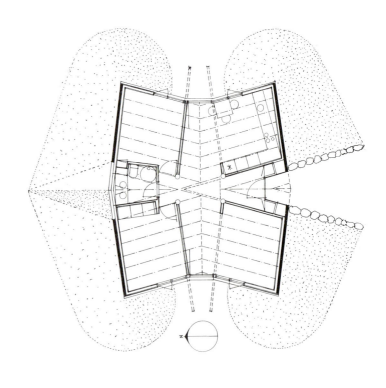

Following ancient techniques of the traditional architecture of northern Europe, the dwelling appears semi-buried in the land. This natural integration allows the wild grass to completely cover the roof structure, leaving only the access zones exposed.

West elevation

South-north section

Cross-section

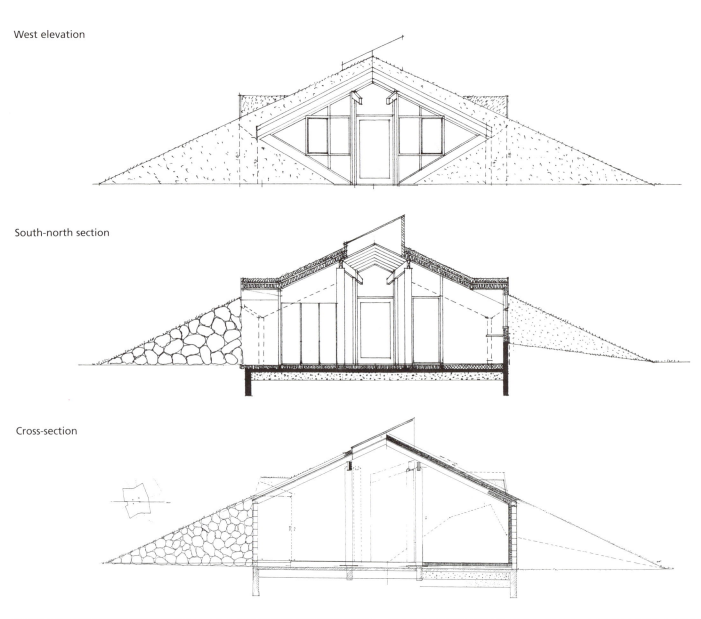

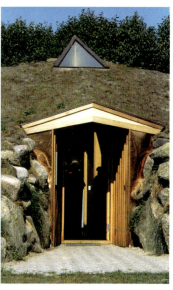

The design of the house is aerodynamic to offer better protection against the weather. To enhance the entrance of natural light, a triangular skylight stands out through the vegetation cover.

Francesco Venezia
House in Posillipo

Naples, Italy

This Neapolitan architect´s subtle approach, based entirely on a topographical and cultural interpretation of the site, is expressed in this small but very detailed project. A cautious but decisive touch lends impact to a domestic interior where function is concealed behind form.
The house stands on a white cliff in Posillipo, occupying a level terrace along a stairway linked to a seaside roadway halfway up the coast. Only interior alterations were made to this pre-existing structure.

A wooden shell shapes the cavity forming the entrance area and living room space; the small entryway opens onto the main living space, kitchen and bedroom.
The wooden walls of the ground floor accommodate a wardrobe and cupboards. The windows, as well as the door onto the small balcony on the side facing the sea, have deep jambs.
The bathroom is at the opposite side of the entrance, excavated in tufa stone. Set in relief within the wall abutting the rock is a recessed fossil of a palm tree.

Photographs: Mimmo Jodice

The narrow entrance opens directly onto the main living area, with the wooden walls accommodating a wardrobe and cupboards.

Shin Takamatsu & Associates
Iwai House

Minami-ku, Japan

Alone in open fields on the edge of town, in an almost defenseless site beyond an industrial belt, stands this two-story private house, built in reinforced concrete and partly steel frame. On both interior and exterior, the architects have brought to bear all the expressive potential of concrete.

The most noticeable feature of the exterior is the curved wall to the left of the entrance on the main facade. Traditionally in architecture, the wall divides inside and out, yet here the curve slowly draws visitors inside and deepens the ambiguity of the relationship between the two. At first glance this convex wall seems rather aggressive, but within the residence its concavity becomes intimate.

The curved wall also forms the outer edge of a secluded courtyard, and incorporates a raised walkway and a terrace from which one can contemplate the scenery. The courtyard and the large windows overlooking it are protected by a brise-soleil.

The glazed entrance hall leads into a sinuous corridor in which the untreated structural concrete creates a fine visual balance with the wooden flooring. Concrete is left unadorned throughout much of the house, for example in the columns, and complements the plastered surfaces, which are mostly white with patches of primary colors.

Absolutely modern though the house is, the interior specially owes a great deal of its delicacy to traditional Japanese aesthetics. The atrium leading to the terrace is a good example of the common ground that exists between the two approaches.

Photographs: Nacása & Partners

Site plan

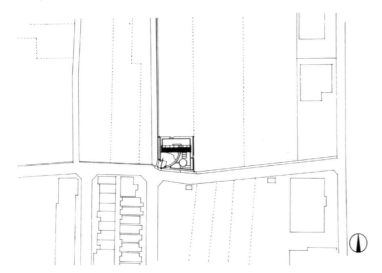

The wide curve not only gives a feeling of protection but also allows the enjoyment of a space at once open, intimate and cool on the ground floor. On the upper level, the elevated walkway and terrace bring sun and civilization closer.

First floor plan

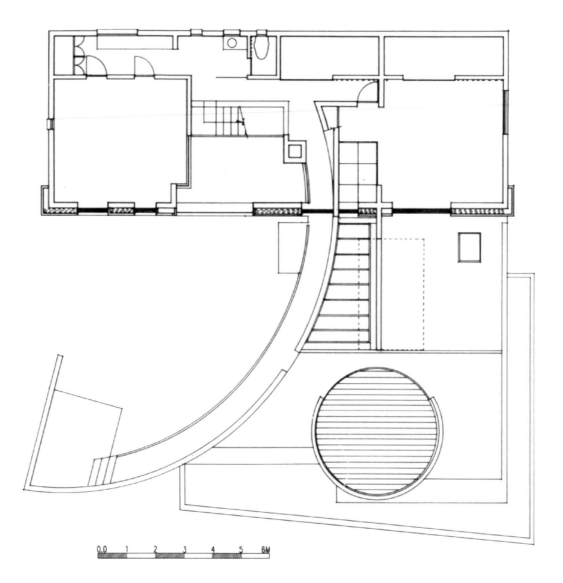

Ground floor plan

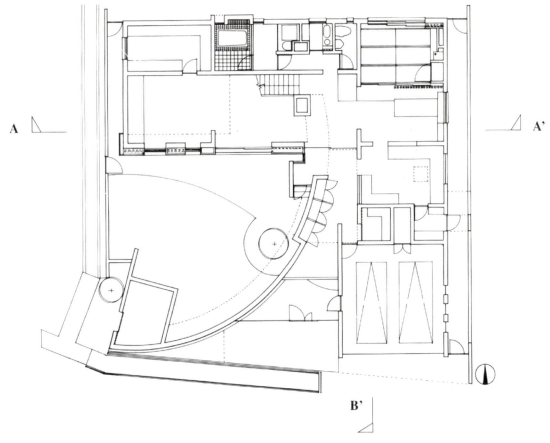

South elevation

East elevation

Section AA'

Section BB'

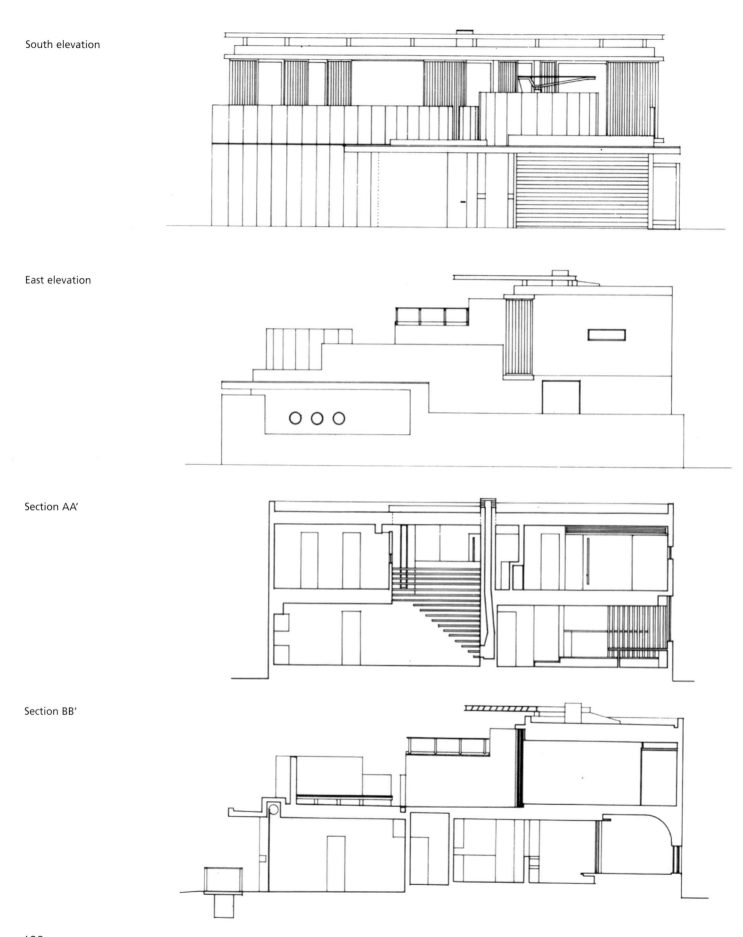

The interior design combines industrial production and traditional detail, rough material and finishes in primary colors.

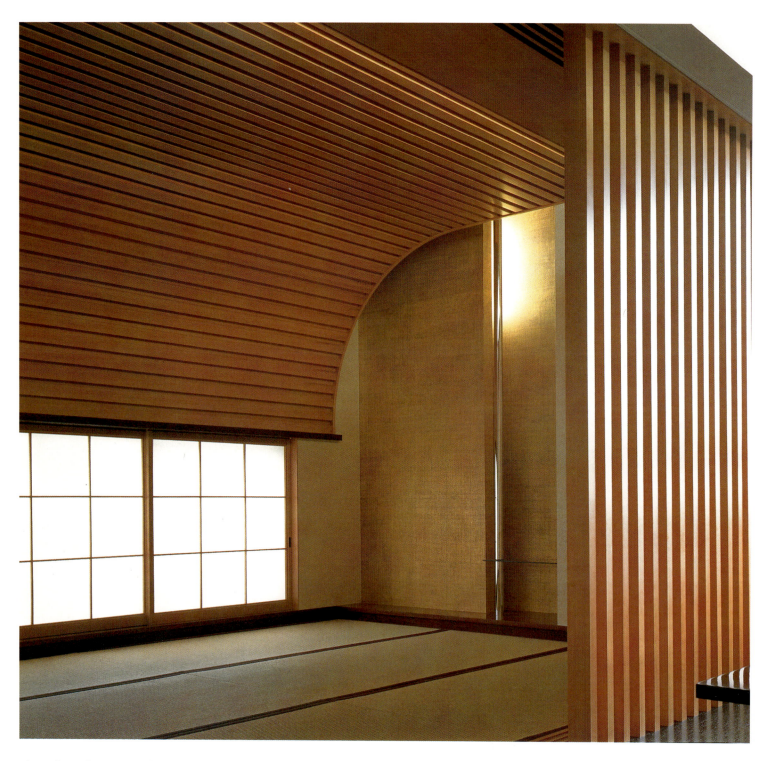

The architect has recreated a typically Oriental atmosphere of serenity in some of the rooms to take refuge from the chaos of Kyoto's outskirts.

"The wall, with its unnatural nature, gradually draws visitors inside, as if they were entering the stomach of Moby Dick". (Shin Takamatsu)

Alvaro Siza
Figueiredo House

Valbom-Gondomar, Portugal

Figueiredo House, in Valbom-Gondomar, is an excellent example of Alvaro Siza's mastery in composing volumes and geometries of great simplicity. The architect's skill lies in the way that he fits them together, creating new forms and physical relations that enhance the quality of the interior spaces and the development of the visual perspectives of the exterior.

This dwelling is located on a small, level plot on one side of the valley where the River Douro crosses the plain on arriving at the city of Oporto. It is arranged on two levels in a symmetric composition based on the intersection of two simple figures: a rectangle, where the greater part of the layout is developed, and an octagon, which establishes a basic structural difference between the two floors.

The ground floor is ordered by the axis of the corridor, around which various rooms are distributed. Here, the upper level octagon can only be discerned by the support columns. The building extends in the form of a ship's prow, opened to the landscape through ample windows.

The octagon plays a dominant role on the upper level. The bedrooms gravitate toward it and the volumetric imbalance that it creates between the levels allowed for a terrace facing the gentle landscape of the valley.

The difference in volumes is also reflected in the facades in the complimentary contrast between the curvature on the lower level and the more severe geometry of the upper level. Nevertheless, the uniform white and the modulation of openings unify the building. Finally, a porch extends from the body of the annex to the entrance of the house.

Photographs: Juan Rodríguez

Ground floor plan

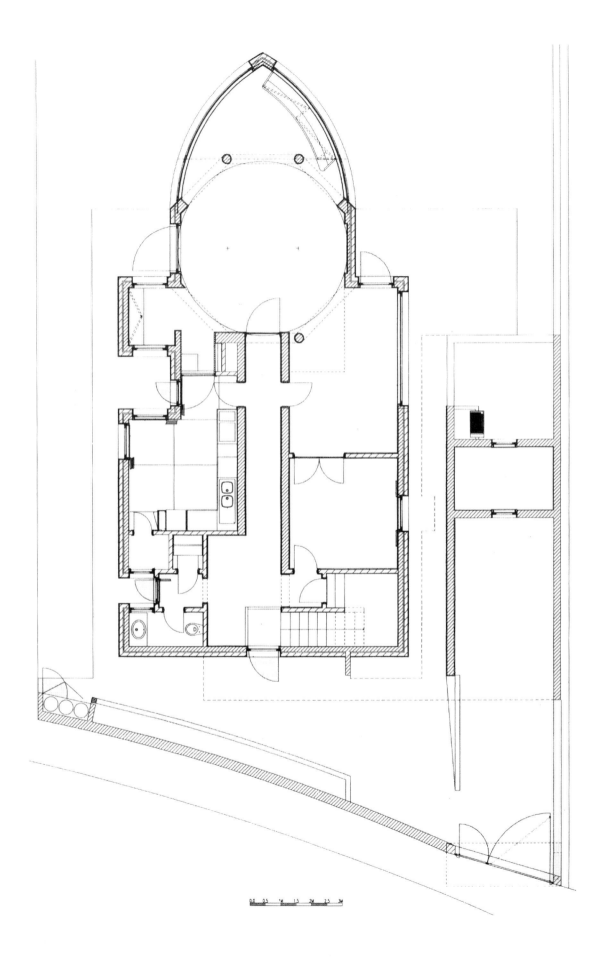

204

The central motif of the relation between building and the site resides in the plastic way in which the building evokes the prow of a ship being steered toward the River Douro from the lawn.

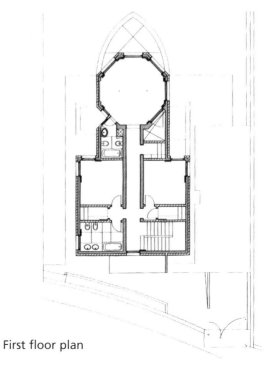

First floor plan

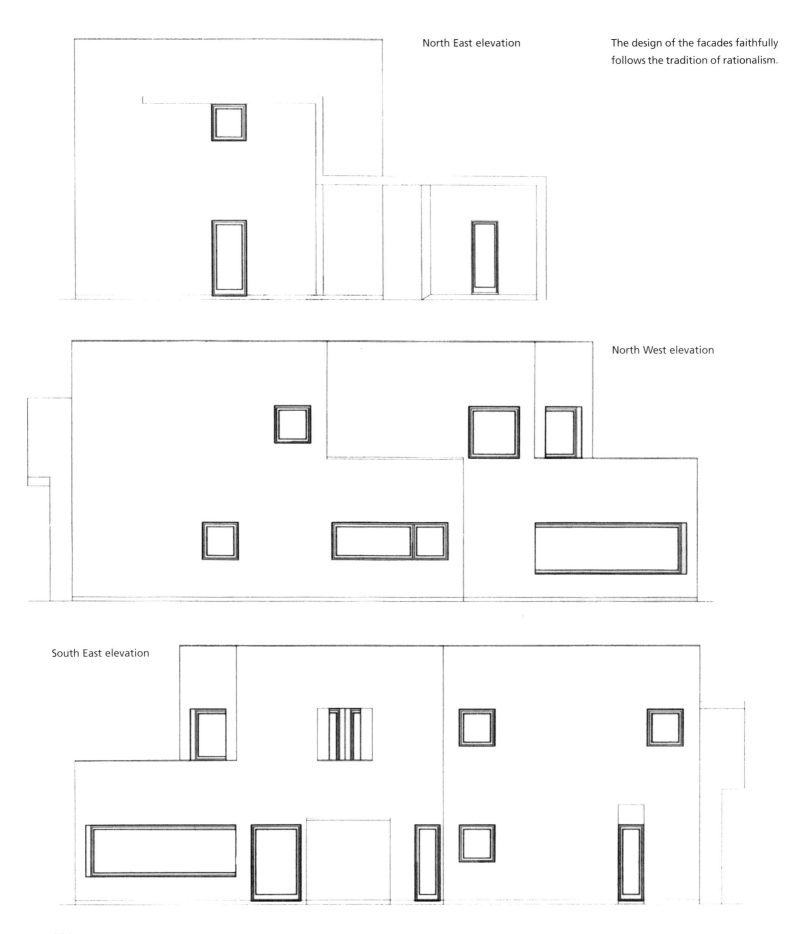

North East elevation

The design of the facades faithfully follows the tradition of rationalism.

North West elevation

South East elevation

The plastic quality of the interior confirms the expressive role of the solution: the curved glass of the large, visually unhindered windows allows a panoramic view of the river and landscape. Blocks of parquet subtly add life to this perception.

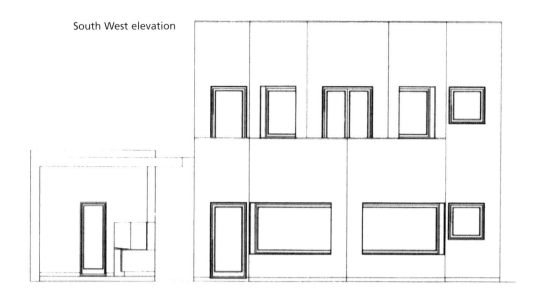
South West elevation

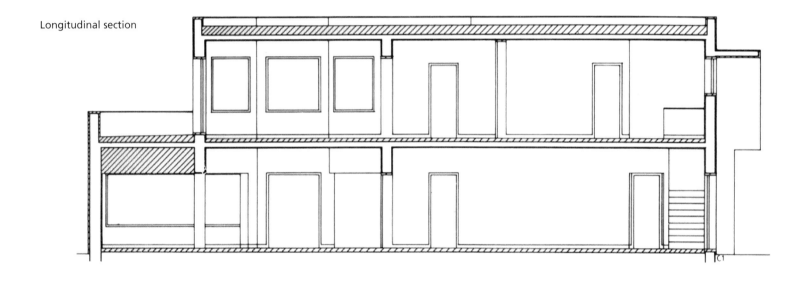
Longitudinal section

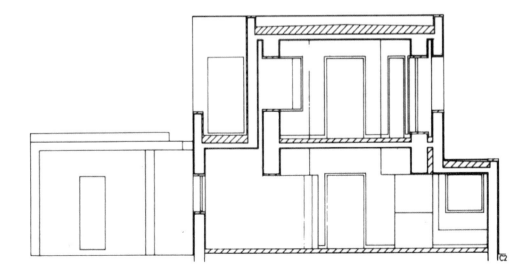
Cross section

Mauro Galantino & Federico Poli (Studio3)
Casa sul lago d'Orta

Orta S Giulio, Italy

This unusual building is located in the Gothic district of an Italian town not far from Milan. The vertical nature of the house is conserved almost intact thanks to the two medieval walls that define the boundaries and the jetty. Before the restoration, the building was in ruins, the ceilings were deteriorated and a large part of the foundations rested on the sandy bed of the lake. According to preliminary research, this building was partly rebuilt in the 14th century, though the jetty was built in the 19th. At first sight, it seems to be a simple rehabilitation. The domestic areas, such as the bedrooms and the living room, are organized vertically in the north "tower", while below the former cowshed, the henhouse, garden and jetty are organized with reference to the lake.

The restoration of this house, which is used as a second residence, respected the stipulations for the conservation of the cultural heritage with regard to volumes, walls and materials.
The work was based on two objectives: to adapt the residential structure to new functions, and to obey the building regulations on the use of materials without sacrificing the possibility of creating a new perception of the rehabilitated parts.
The result was a residential space composed of a double-height living room forming a horizontal, parallelepiped space with a covered jetty at the south end and a structure containing the living areas at the other end.

Photographs: Alberto Muciaccia

The staircase communicates the floors of the "tower", which houses the bedroom and which is located at the north end of the residence. At the south end, the jetty juts out onto Lake Orta.

The jetty acts as an entrance door to this "residential microcosm". It was built in the 19th century to extend the horizontal volume of this medieval building.

Ground floor plan

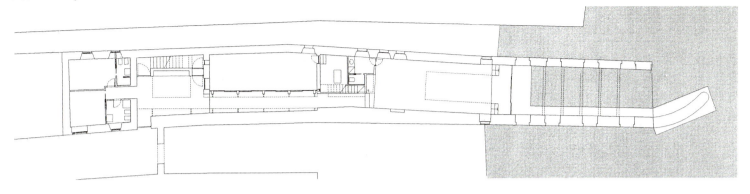

First floor plan

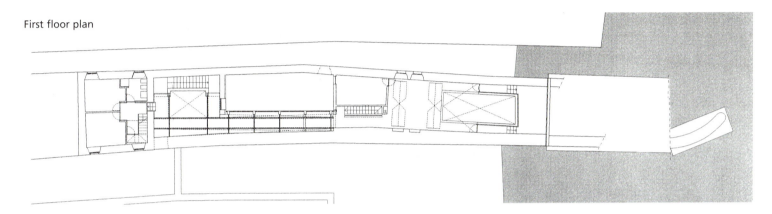

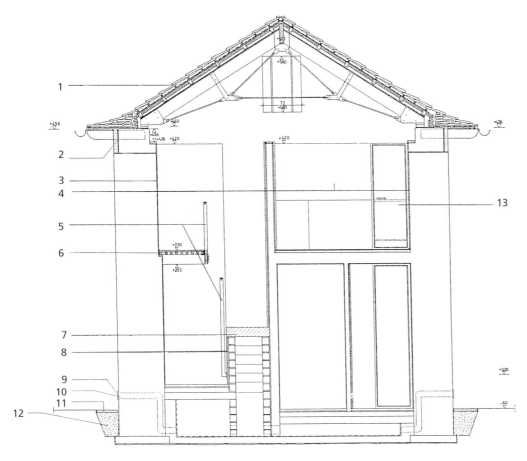

Section of living room

1 Roof
2 Unpolished gneiss cornice
3 Plaster-type facing with vermiculite
4 Cladding of horizontal polished gneiss panels
5 Varnished steel railing, 4x4 "T" horizontal, 4x4 "H" vertical
6 5x5x5 grill
7 Staircase with polished solid gneiss steps on hollow-brick partitions
8 Cladding of horizontal polished gneiss panels
9 Protection grill
10 Breather of the ventilated floor
11 Unpolished gneiss tile
12 Gravel
13 Wall with 6/6/4 double glazing and varnished galvanized steel frame

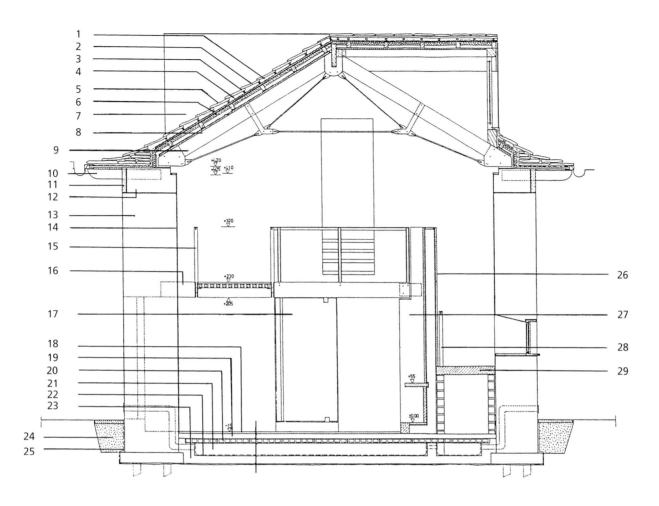

Section of atrium

1. Vapor barrier
2. Unpolished gneiss
3. 4x4 gneiss fixing strips
4. Hot-welded butyl layer, 4x15 strips
5. Nailed 5 cm larch floorboards
6. Rock wool insulation
7. Panels of several layers of wood with oak on the inside
8. Oak dimensioning beams
9. Truss
10. Copper eaves
11. Chestnut corbel
12. Unpolished gneiss tile
13. Existing building
14. Unpolished gneiss tile
15. Varnished steel railing, 4x4 "T" horizontal, 4x4 "H" vertical
16. Varnished steel face
17. Opaline glass door
18. Polished gneiss floor
19. Carpet
20. Large clay floor tiles
21. Partition
22. Polyethylene sheets
23. Weak-mix concrete
24. Gravel
25. Polyethylene sheets
26. Polished gneiss cladding
27. Solid gneiss pilaster
28. Railing
29. Solid polished gneiss steps

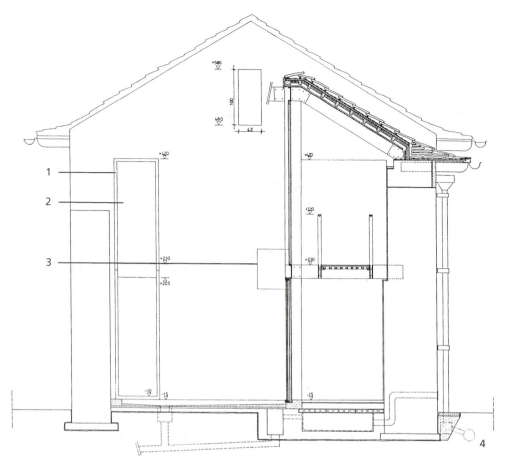

Section through gallery

1 Gneiss profile
2 Varnished galvanised iron wall 4/6/4
3 Wall
4 Rainwater

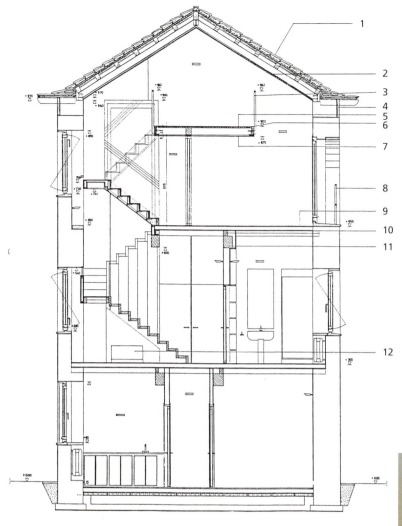

Section through building

1 Roof
2 2.5 cm oak-veneered plywood boards
3 Railing
4 Unpolished gneiss tile
5 Teak boards
6 Floorboards
7 Drop ceiling of 2-5 cm oak-finish plywood boards
8 Iron wall, "H" 4x4 horizontal, "T" 4x4 vertical
9 Teak boards
10 Oak floorboards
11 Oak beam
12 Fancoil

The staircase communicates the floors of the "tower" located at the north end of the residence which houses the bedroom. At the south end is the jetty on Lake Orta.

Mutsue Hayakusa (Cell Space Architects)
Fold House

Nagareyama, Chiba, Japan

The composition of this small residence for a young couple and two dogs consists of three manipulations: layering, wrapping, and shifting. Different architectural materials have been wrapped in layers in order to create the family's living space as a series of veils.

First, thin sheets of paper were layered and rolled; then they were bent to form angles. Because they lack stability as they were, they were squashed sideways and linked to one another. They were shifted along the south-north axis, so that sunlight is intercepted during summer and drawn inside during winter.

The family does not use chairs: they live on the floor. Inclined planes are backrests; walls are furniture.

According to the architect, building a small house is like spinning a thread from the residents' living habits, sense of values and environment and then tailoring a huge garment to be worn collectively. This is why square, rigid elements have been kept to a minimum here. The idea was to create a dwelling with just enough strength to weather wind and rain, enveloped in soft layers, one which would be a house and furniture at the same time.

Photographs: Satoshi Asakawa

Site plan

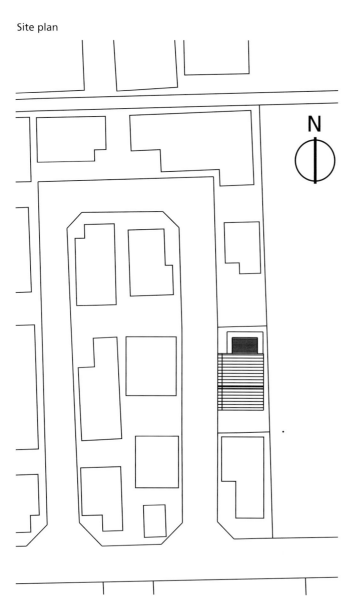

Huge eaves and a terrace were arranged on the southern side. Here, a large space accommodates gatherings, while the smaller spaces house the entrance and water utilities. There are two staircases, one outside and one inside.

First floor plan

1 Bedroom
2 Garage

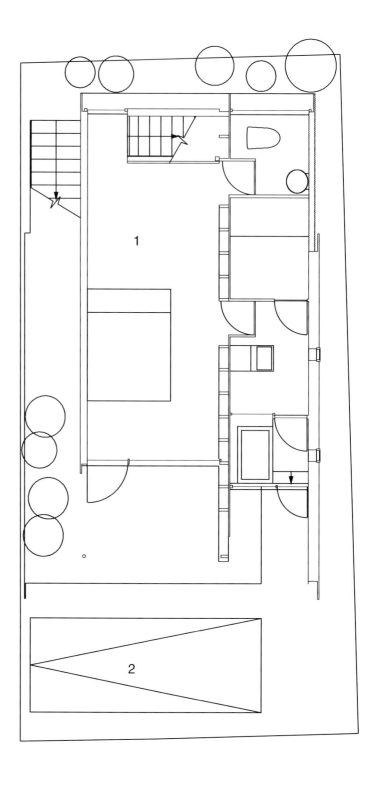

Second floor plan

3 Entrance
4 Kitchen
5 Living room
6 Terrace 1

Loft floor plan

7 Loft
8 Terrace 2

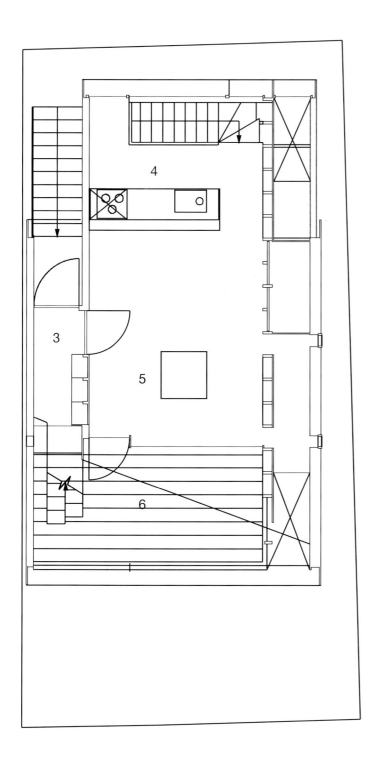
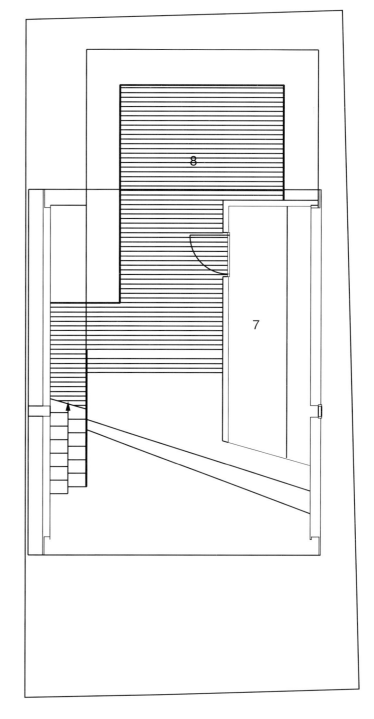

North elevation

South elevation

East elevation   West elevation

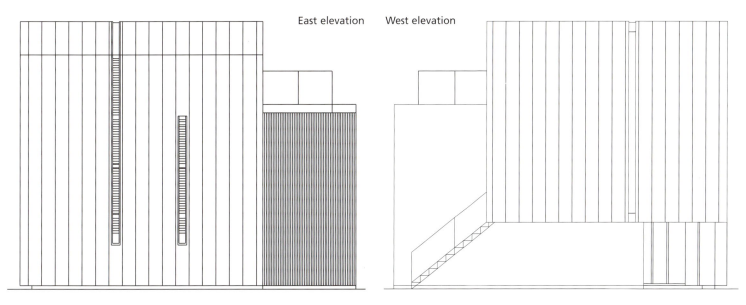

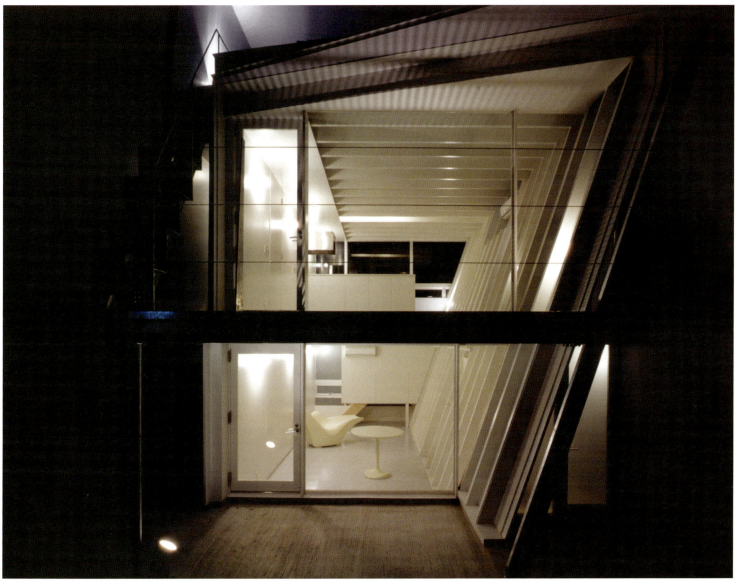

Sections

1 Bedroom
4 Kitchen
5 Living room
6 Terrace 1
7 Loft
8 Terrace 2

Silvia Gmür & Livio Vacchini
3 Single–Family Houses

Beinwil am See, Canton Argovia, Switzerland

Located in the Swiss town of Beinwil am see these three single-family modules stand out from the architecture of the area due to their special design and arrangement. Three identical dwellings located on a hillside with a view of the lake give form to a single complex. The different modules share their foundations in a kind of pedestal that determines part of their architectural character, enhancing their role in the landscape. The dwellings create a compositional rhythm in which the predominant geometry of the floors is the square, whereas in the elevations it is the rectangle. This rhythm is determined by a linear succession of "solids" and "voids" in which the former act as private spaces while the latter are used for the common living areas. The private space is divided in turn into porch and room, so the differentiation between exterior and interior is slightly blurred.

The facades are composed of three differentiated elements that are used for their functionality and their aesthetic qualities: cement, glass and "air" that in the void is converted into matter. It is an architecture that tends towards the essential without expressive rhetoric or metaphoric language, an architecture without superfluous details in which the orientation becomes crucial through its form, structures and materials.

The generous use of natural light, a perfect organization of the spaces, the choice of specific materials, and the careful orientation of the structures are the basic ingredients of this well-organized, balanced work. These three dwellings not only produce multiplicity, variety, potentiality and virtuality, but also a way of inhabiting and combining private and common spaces.

Photographs: Vaclav Sedy

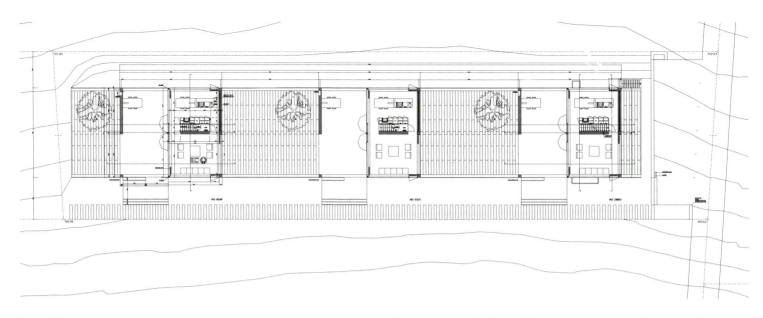

Ground floor plan

The elementary rhythm of the square-cube is added to the horizontal nature of the base on which the three dwellings are placed, creating an expressive and symphonic effect in which the different dimensions seem to mediate between the vertical and the horizontal, and between the solid and the void.

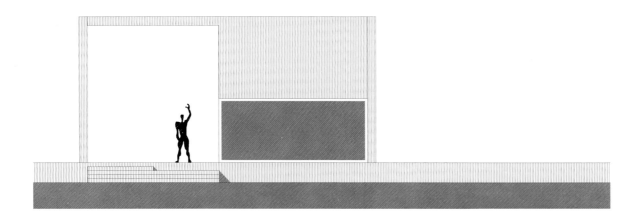

Elevation

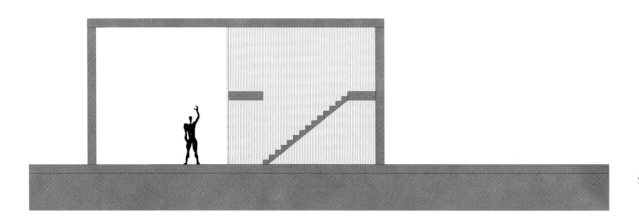

Section

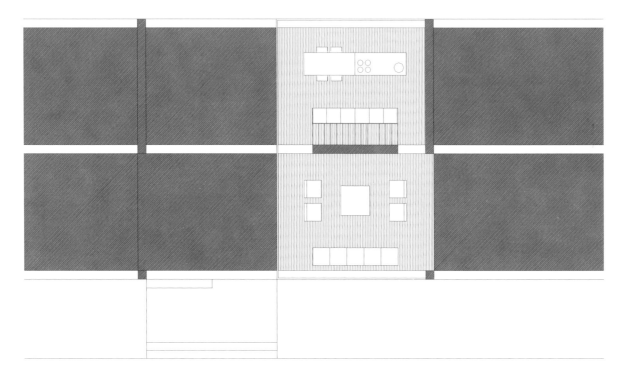

Floor plan

North-east elevation

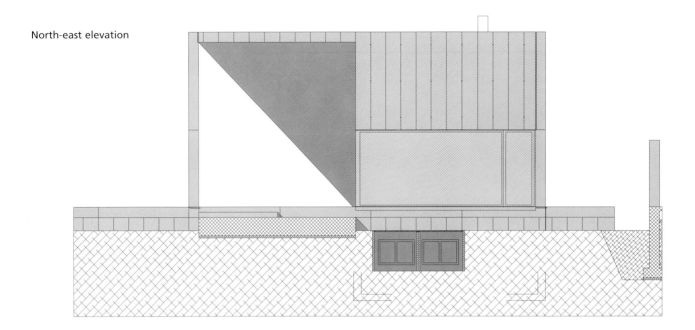

South-west elevation

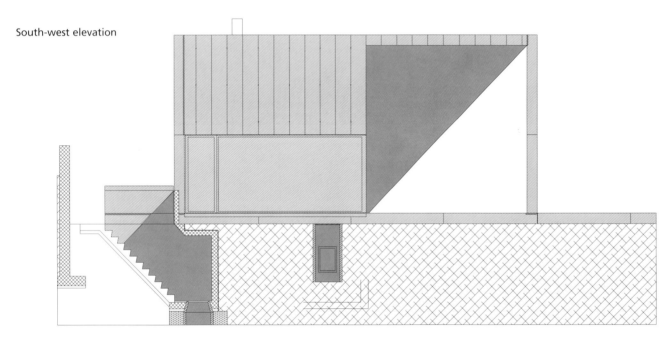

South-east elevation North-west elevation

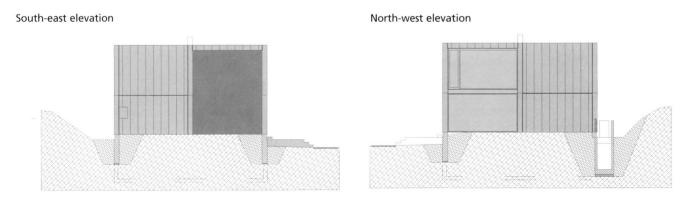

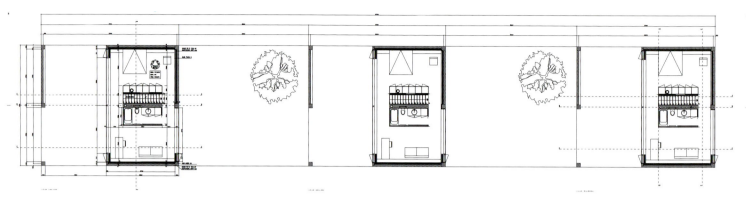

First floor plan

In the interior, the three dwellings have the same simple and functional layout. The kitchen-dining room and the living room are located at ground level, while on the upper floor a large bedroom occupies the entire space with the exception of a central module containing a bathroom, a fitted cupboard and the stairwell.

Takao Shiotsuka
N Guest House

Oita, Japan

This guesthouse, which is set in a small cove and surrounded by natural woodland, enjoys a splendid view of the sea for as far as the eye reaches. It was commissioned by the owners of the adjacent factory as a restful place where visitors could stay, dine or lie down for a while.

Because of its ideal location overlooking the bay, a prime consideration in the design was ensuring ample views toward the sea. Thus, the entire sea-facing façade is glazed, with a large opening measuring 4 meters in height and 5 meters in width. In order to keep the view as unobstructed as possible, all necessary circulation routes and service areas have been grouped together at the far end of this basically rectangular floor plan (ie, the end where the entrance is located).

The exterior seascape seems to be drawn into the house by the choice of marine colors and with the walls and ceiling coated in glossy paint that reflects the natural light and the glimmers refracted off the water.

While a view of the sea was a central design theme, it was equally important to ensure a sense of privacy. Aside from the glazed front of the building, there are very few windows in the rest of the house. The dark, tinted glass at the entrance keeps anyone approaching the house from seeing into the interior.

The completely blind side walls, while ensuring privacy, also shield visitors from unwanted views of the factory sitting just next door and serve as a noise barrier.

Photographs: Kaori Ichikawa

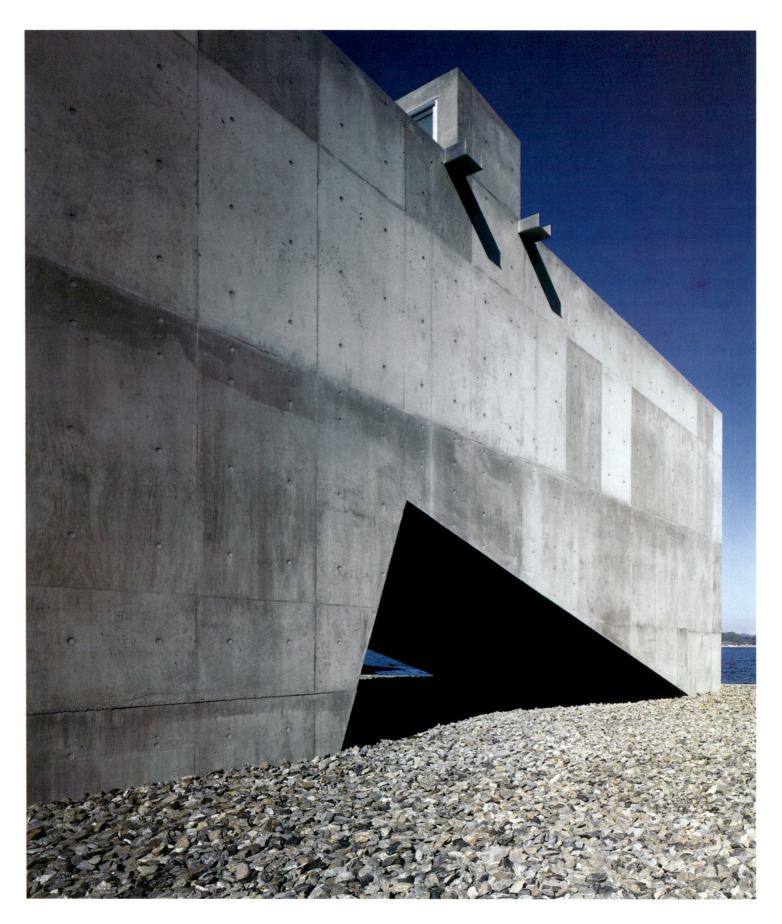

First floor plan

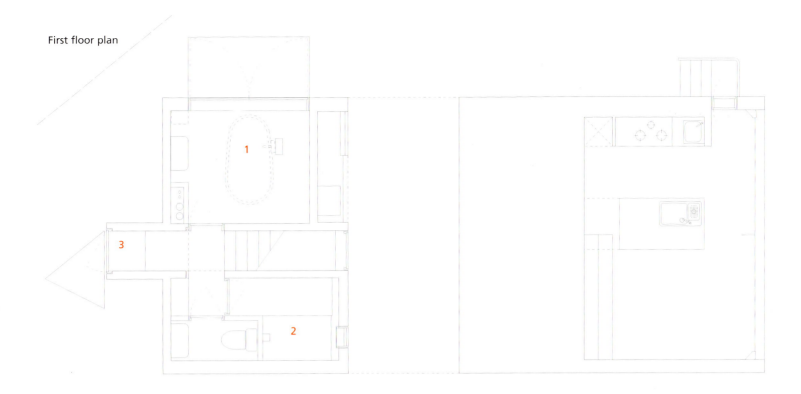

Visitors at the guesthouse are hardly aware that there is a factory next door. The thick concrete exterior walls dampen the sound of the factory, while a complete absence of windows on the side walls keeps out unwanted views. A massive 4 X 5 meter opening toward the sea, however, provides calming views and abundant light.

Second floor plan

1 Bathroom
2 Shower room
3 Entrance
4 Lounge

Section

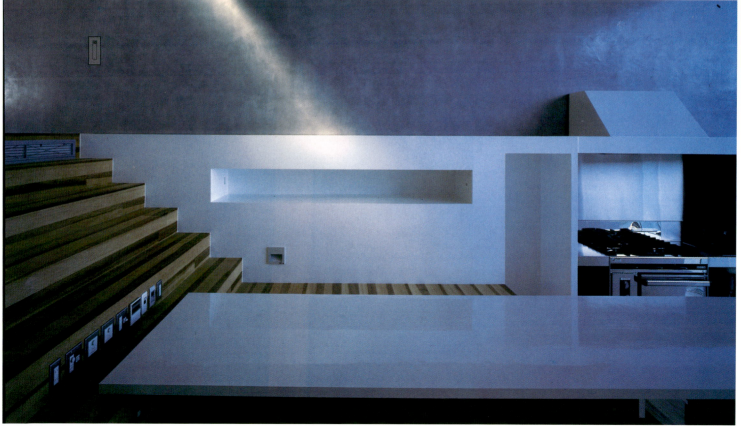